Against the Evidence

David Ignatow

Against the Evidence

SELECTED

POEMS

1934–1994

Wesleyan University Press

Published by University Press of New England

Hanover and London

Wesleyan University Press

Published by University Press of New England, Hanover, NH 03755

© 1993 by David Ignatow

Printed in the United States of America 5 4 3 2 1

CIP data appear at the end of the book

Poems appearing in this volume have been published previously in:

New and Collected Poems, 1970–1985, © 1975, 1978, 1984, 1986

Poems, 1934–1969, © 1946, 1948, 1953, 1955, 1956, 1957, 1958, 1959, 1960, 1961, 1962, 1963, 1964, 1965, 1966, 1967, 1968, 1969, 1970

Selected Poems, © 1948, 1955, 1956, 1960, 1961, 1962, 1963, 1964, 1965, 1966, 1967, 1968, 1969, 1970

Shadowing the Ground, © 1991

"Despite the Plainness of the Day," "Orgasm," "Opening Paths," "See," "You," "My Love for You," "Each of us," "Now," "Blood," "I Dream I Hurl a Spear," "Midnight II," "Shapely," "The Wound," "The Mask," "Without Sexual Attraction," "The Puzzle," and "The Life," reprinted by permission of Mill Hunk Books from *Despite the Plainness of the Day: Love Poems* by David Ignatow, edited by Anthony Petrosky and Peter Oresick. © 1991 by David Ignatow.

CONTENTS

III. Poems of the 1950s

IV. Poems of the 1960s

V. Poems of the 1970s

FROM *Tread the Dark* (1978)

VI. Poems of the 1980s

VII. Poems of the 1990s

FROM *Despite the Plainness of the Day: Love Poems* (1991)

The reader of *Against the Evidence: Selected Poems 1934–1994* will discover that, unlike the arrangement of poems in the separate volumes according to theme—as in *Rescue the Dead* and in books of the seventies, *Facing the Tree* being the first of these—in the present volume I have brought poems together according to the decade in which they were written. My practice, in gathering poems to complete or advance a theme, was, where needed, to gather work supporting the theme from different decades, overlooking the time in which they were written. Not a few poems were taken out of their original order. But I must say that under no circumstance was a theme decided on in advance. Rather, the body of work on which I based the organization spoke to me of its overriding concerns. I am referring to poems conceived within a particular period that gave them their consistency of tone and style. To this major group I would add work that in itself, apart from the period in which it belongs, entered into the thought. Unquestionably, this practice meant that my writing was an organic whole from the start of my writing career. That view has not changed for me. But now, in placing each poem in its proper time, I am returning each to its chronological order.

Through the years, I did notice the evident difference of style and tone in the poems taken from earlier decades in contrast with the more recent work, and I did promise myself that there would come a time when I could explain, if only to satisfy myself, my innate sense of a somewhat fractured whole beneath the surface of my concentration on theme at that time. I would explain and also correct.

The opportunity to make this correction arrived when *Selected Poems*, meaningfully edited by Robert Bly, became limited in relation to my first seventies volume, *Facing the Tree*, followed soon after by *Tread the Dark*. Bly's editing had had to limit itself to the sixties. The two new books of the seventies signaled a new style and tone in contrast with the language of realism, though it was in the lyric mode in which the earlier poems had been written. Strangely, my first considered reaction to this difference was to think that I had created a dichotomy for myself between the two modes, with my sense and need of continuity put to the question. Later, returning to study the change more closely and having pondered it, I came to recognize that both styles, after all, were treating the same subjects. The reader, however, would find himself facing the same puzzlement as I did, and so I decided to put together this updated, revised selection, with the explanation that would, or could, content the reader and myself, in particular.

So, having discovered that I was writing on the same subjects in two conflicting, or apparently conflicting, styles, I was thrown back upon myself as the ultimate clarifier. The new mode was in the tradition of both the symbolic and the mythic, especially those invented by me. And I realized that, after all, I had been writing in these two modes in the three Ritual poems and a small number of scattered poems, all in *Poems 1934–1969*, in other words, in the fifties and sixties. That I had published these in that early collection could mean only that, not attempting to be different, I was then already seeking for meaning not limited to the event itself as demanded by realistic techniques. The writing of symbol and myth by its very nature was freed of the limitations of reality and could lend an incident or incidents conjectures of meaning wider than was possible in the language of realism. In brief, as can be seen in *New and Collected Poems, 1970–1985*, I was seeking an explanation, if one existed, for the anger and passion I experienced in myself that spurred my earlier writing to portray the unhappy state of life, not only for myself but for others around me. If this was to be what life consisted of, then, in desperation, there was the need to fathom the nature of such an atrocity within ourselves, or at least to venture in that direction before letting oneself sink into despair, and to escape it and if possible to resolve it.

I should mention that humor with which those very scarifying themes are treated from time to time, perhaps as a kind of side play; for relief and affirmation make it possible to play with danger to one's satisfaction in prevailing through humor. The reader will find such moments interspersed where I felt they could not only break the somber mood but also lift the spirit to see that it and it alone is paramount in the life of being. Humor about living is implicit to my state of mind. May it have a bearing upon the reader's thoughts and pleasure in the face of the uncertainties of our time. There also is love.

The reader may want to go back to the single books where the poems are arranged to realize themes, which encompass all I have wanted to say and portray in organized, disciplined meaning. That in itself may be of interest and of worth. I still stand by these books, but arranging work according to decade, at least of the actual events of the particular decade, is another order of experience for me. That is, the poems, each in their decade, as a body offer a cross section and, I believe, an in-depth portrait of life and living of that particular time, allowing the authenticity of the whole that was not possible and was not the objective in the books thematically arranged. They had their own truths to tell. For me, they form a complete statement to which I hold with gratitude for having written to achieve my own sense of being and place. For *Against the Evidence* I have gathered from the most resonant of my work. The poems speak of sixty years of a contribution to American poetry, the significance of which awaits judgment.

A word about a small number of poems revised since their first publication: I'm sure I have clarified and strengthened them.

To Jeannette Hopkins and Virginia Terris, I am deeply indebted for their perspicacity and suggestions that were crucial in shaping the book in its present form.

D.I.

I

Poems of the 1930s

Adolescence

I too have been drawn in
by a silken cord hung from her waist,
my form clapped to hers
and freedom restrained to our movement together.
Caught and the fields at our backs
we look past each other's face
but see our stretched necks
and taut cheeks straining.

Is this the love I ran after,
crying to it to turn
and catch me up? Whoever I chased
ran over the length of the world.

The Folk Singer

The other day I heard in the movies
a man sing a song, just like he told
your own troubles; he sang so beautiful,
just like you feel it,
it was just like in life: your ambitions
when you're young, and end up
in a shoe store; it was so good,
and everybody clapped
as if he could hear from the screen,
it was so beautiful
how he sang.

For a Friend

I did not tell you to open the window
when the sun shines. I asked for an old man
near a tattered cart selling luck charms.
But tell me, what is the truth,
what is the music in the box
when bananas fall from stars?
I would not peel a stinking egg
if I were you, Columbus, O Gem of the ocean.
Make it stand without breaking.

I said the rain was running against the curb
and the clop of hooves in the air,
fuzzy light, wet walks;
your clothes all wet.
I said you must not turn your back
nor take away your hands.
You must not humph, nor drop your clothes from you
and leave the room.
                              You left and not even a handshake
while the factory whistled come to work.
I turned in bed going over the ground with you
and agreeing. In the dawn I rose
looking for needle and thread.
I found a dime in the street.

Neighbors

Where do they find the answers?
Never have I heard shouting or violent noise
from the windows across the street. Lights
and music, some loud talk, glasses tinkling
and cigar smoke trailing out the windows.
I will not say perfect lives,
I have heard of the death of a daughter
in childbirth. The tears and laments
were hard to listen to, people closed
their windows and wiped their brows.

The grandmother sits silently
on the stoop with the newborn.
Here is quiet and ability to dress
and undress, to eat and to digest,
to expel waste and to make arrangements
and to carry them out.

For My Mother Ill

I'll join you in your sleep,
into the same darkness dive,
where dead fish float together.
But we shall be communing,
blindly and without feeling,
by knowing now,
as I lie back upon a pillow,
as you close your eyes,
its comfort.

II

Poems
of the
1940s

Birthday

Today being the day, what gift can I give
myself, earth giving none, nor my nearest
relative? I take the gift of coming bombs.
We shall all be dead on a certain day.
I take my last few looks at the surrounding
scene: stone buildings, hard pavements,
noisy streets, trees dying
of carbon dioxide.
                    May I live to see
this last bomb flower
in the paradise we promised to each other.

The Murderer

I pull a knife but it is to protest
a loss. I am not allowed to love
that person who has made me angry.
Is this then what he wants?
He has this blade to find out his heart;
and those who cart me off to jail,
I love them too
for the grief and anger
I have given.

Consolation

My wife, I dread to come and tell you
how we've failed. It is not our doing
wholly. What has gone out of us
is the impelling reason to succeed,
to set ourselves above others,
to live more perfectly. All this

has left us as though we too
had been possessed of a fever,
and our minds now turning cool
have revealed to us our arms
enclosed about each other.

Money and Grass

1

Tonight reality is in the rest
I have found from murdering myself
racing through streets,
my mind racing ahead,
my body pounding after
money—green as grass!

No time to think of grass!
No time to think of lying under a tree,
watching people far off in a slow-motion
drama towards each other.

2

Tonight,
I have stuffed wax into my ears
to keep out the trucks and auto horns
in the street. I listen to my blood
ringing until it sounds like crickets
in a woods at night. I am quieted,
listening to my own isolation,
myself rooted in the compact,
the quality of earth held in a full hand,
the silkiness, the tiny workworms,
the little stones and the rootbeer deliciousness
of the earth itself, brown, black or red
for growing.
　　　　　I feel through my cricket-singing
blood and rest my underlying constant affair

with earth, with its trees that are tall
and pregnant to express love, and the grass
running with the wind: the happiness
one must bring to love and the clumps
of flower bushes the occasional monuments
one must leave to love. I feel love only
can be justice, and the earth grow it.

I feel never to leave this perfect lover,
and roll upon it with the abandonment
of a lover on his mistress' body.
I get up renewed in having released myself,
the tiredness and tingling gone with it,
and I am earth's offering again
to wild horns and engines.

The White Ceiling

Until that child, one flight below, stops crying,
struck by its mother, I cannot sleep—
until it is hushed up by kindness,
a stroke silently, softly given upon its head.
Why not, I think, go downstairs in my bathrobe,
knock gently on the door and ask permission,
"If you don't mind," so that I too
may sleep.
            There was an argument
between parents about money; not altogether;
their voices personal as money is not.
In the hush of an unhappy truce the slap sounded.
Since those below are helpless, I lie here
and look up at the white ceiling.

A Working Principle

Let them go around on tiptoes,
craning their necks for the ineffable
in the driving rain, as flatfooted and slow,
I make my way, unable to pretend
as others do, maddened at the prospect
before them, that beauty calls them
from within. I will end in the mud,
face down, saying the night is dark.
They will say, Black is merely the absence
of color.

Subway

There slouched the drunk, head fallen
to a side, arms hung down. I strode by
to take a seat farther up the train
though I was tired and had determined
to be settled in the first vacancy.
I kept walking, revolted. Here all day
I had worked to make better a portion
of my life—to find him at my feet.
I should have sat down opposite
and confessed that if this day
really were bettered by my efforts
he could not deter me.

Crowding

So many are dead or dying
that I begin to think
it must be right;
and so many are
crowding into the world
that living too
must be worthwhile.

Premonitions

A bird winging through space
you love for the distance
it soars and circles
in time.

In places where the sun does not reach,
in a shady room, time presses again
upon the forehead. In a field
under a shady tree it comes
softly to rest upon your head.
You dread the first sight
of the going down of the sun,
the air melancholy over the fields,
the sky thoughtful and subdued upon the hills,
the trees prominent and stark.
But this melancholy you enjoy,
feeling its richness of the sun,
is time again, returning, I think,
in sympathy.
        For time,
I begin to believe, is the earth
pressing upwards against our feet,
our heads to feel it that the sun softens,
its message that we are one.

Time then is the warning of death to come,
pressing upon us in a shaded room
or under a shady tree and at night
when the sun must leave us to darkness,
for the sun too by this token
is in time's control.
        Then time
has its deceptions for us in the sun
and we are time itself running its course,
and when done, time remains as earth
and we are dying to be born into the world

again for we are thoughts of time
and our shapes too are time and because
all things are one
with their differences
which add up to time.

And so we are not alone dying
and not alone being born,
earth's weight urging upon us
in one pressure of life and death.
Time then for us is a standing still
in abundance, so much so
that it is all and we are in eternity.
And what we do for now is for always,
as what we have done is the future too
which is always.

FROM Poems (1948)

Statement for the Times

On Sunday, day of rest, I stroll the park,
visiting the lake and the ducks in it.
I look at the hills in the distance
in another state. I go home,
I go to war with my ambition against my mind.

The larger wars are for the masses.
They will burn down the cities
and build them up again.
They will burn them down again
and be damned for it
but they will build them up
for a stubborn ideal.

Peace for Awhile

Peace for awhile,
but there is no such thing as peace forever.
The calm suburbs you see
while passing by on a train,
the children riding their bikes under trees,
are only interludes between the strain
of coming to grips with what we wish to do
and the failure to do it.

Poem

I am tired of you
as I am tired of myself.
There is a mountain I am climbing
in the dark,
and when I reach its top
the dark will be there.

Harold

From the west comes Harold, with a bitter smile,
and a dry hate in his voice for micks, wops,
kikes and refugees.
                        Too bad he has to work
in a Jewish hospital, admitting Jewish people,
sick or ready to give birth. He makes sure
not to raise his head while women suffer
before him as he writes slowly his data.
Or else how could he write home to the West,
to the tall sombreros and the spittin' type
that he, the climax of a pioneering dream,
works for Jews to make his bread?
Where is the gun he ought to pull
to plug them all, then swing off at a canter
for parts unknown till things cool off,

still master of his fate and fortune,
his own?
Here he mouths blasphemous phrases,
shocking his own Baptist soul. He makes free
with farts, shoots his jibes,
orders the help around.

He laces it into the assistant director,
the biggest, bloatiest doctor of them all,
and takes his something bucks a week disdainfully
for rent, food, gas to keep a car
and six-cent stamp for home.

Europe and America

My father brought the emigrant bundle
of desperation and worn threads,
that in anxiety as he stumbles
tumble out distractedly;
while I am bedded upon soft green money
that grows like grass.
Thus, between my father
who lives on bed of anguish for his daily bread,
and I who tear money at leisure by the roots,
where I lie in sun or shade,
a vast continent of breezes, storms to him,
shadows, darkness to him, small lakes, rough channels:
to him, and hills, mountains to him, lie between us.

My father comes of a small hell
where bread and man have been kneaded and baked together.
You have heard the scream as the knife fell;
while I have slept
as guns pounded offshore.

Nurse

The old man who can undress before you
as easily as before a mirror believes
that you are only the matured concept of his body,
as idea only.

Let us hope your uniform does not deceive him,
in that you are dedicated to his care.
The dress you wear is white for the abolition
of all your woes before his;
for he has worn the body of his time
a little longer and a little more indulgently
than you, whose cries of welcome or goodby
beneath his window on your night leave
will wake him fitfully from the dream
of the burden of earth given back to earth again.

You are to know that body is love
of having been born and to grow old
is to be born into returning to the good
from which he came.
You have eyes to see no shame
but resignation in his stooped figure,
such as love brings.

And now, your own eyes are colorless of wrong,
and every look is to follow
one man's devotion to being old.
You take his clothes from him,
and let him rest;
and in your going to and fro
from cabinet to cot carry instruments
of your respect to his side.

Get the Gasworks

Get the gasworks in a poem
and you've got the smoke and smokestacks,
the mottled red and yellow tenements,
and grimy kids who curse with the pungency
of the odor of gas. You've got America, boy.

Sketch in the river, and barges,
all dirty and slimy.
How do the seagulls stay so white?
And always cawing like little mad geniuses?
You've got the kind of living
that makes the kind of thinking we do:
gaswork smokestack whistle tooting wisecracks.

They don't come because we like it that way,
but because we find it outside our window every morning,
in soot on the furniture,
and trucks carrying coal for gas,
the kid hot after the ball under the wheel.
He gets it over the belly, alright.
He lies there.

So the kids keep tossing the ball around
after the funeral.
So the cops keep chasing them,
so the mamas keep hollering,
and papa flings his newspaper outward,
in disgust with discipline.

Come!

Come, let us blow up the whole business;
the city is insane.
Let us plant trees, grass and flowers
in the rubble to disguise it.

Let us restore the city to its first aim
of being natural to the touch.

Break down the sordid hospital,
the cockroach-ridden restaurants,
the whore-packed hotels
and business buildings close by for convenience;
the big night clubs and intimate ones
in the cellars of old homes,
where rats and vermin and dark dampness
used to sport.

The stock exchange and the banks
where we sell each other;
the gaudy apartment houses and the broken-down ones
to which we have been assigned,
each according to his profit;
the gutters where we run each other down;
the sidewalks where we watch with interest.
The stores of adulterated foods
and ready medicines;
the hospitals with an eye towards business
and the doctor's income;
the homes for the aged
where the aged are forgotten.
All this let us demolish once and for all
with a perfect time bomb;
and of course with the formality of a warning
to those who will wish to stay behind.
But let us wipe out a few hundred million.

East Side West

The stairs squeak like mice caught outside
their holes. I notice the stained brown door
of my neighbor, perhaps the one whose mailbox
I have envied, packed full like a suckling pig.

The door sounds with life behind it,
the door seems to speak: a mother shrieks
at her youngest daughter, snaps at her next
oldest child, grumbles to herself
of the work, curses the whole bunch around her.
"Kids, kids!" She needs help, lonely for help.
A mother, I recall, of four, her hair
braided around hawk features. Trailed
by these four ducklings, she lugs shopping bags
in both hands up five flights. The good husband
every night at six races up the stairs
and his rat-tat on the door demands entrance
into his rightful troubles. The door closes
behind him and begins to sound with a new tune:
money, the bosses, the working conditions,
the other workers. Stinks, all stinks.
He is lonely for help.

I turn the corner to this first floor carefully
so as not to be heard having stood so long
in the hall listening. Up on the next floor
a radio croons with a practiced, honeyed voice.
A young girl moans with it off key.
She too takes care of a house, her mother dead,
one baby sister left behind, four grown brothers
busy on street corners shooting craps.
The baby cries and she snaps at it.
I have seen her look long passing me
on the stairs, as if searching in me
for the help she needs.

III

Poems
of the
1950s

Old

The wonder is mine as she counts
the two trees, the two boys and girls.
I am childlike as I listen.
How old am I, I ask,
and the lack of money
to haunt me?
Will I never grow to earn
a living for us both
in ease and plenitude?
Will I always lack the strength
to stand alone? I tighten
my grip on her in my arms
at the open window;
I am growing old.

An Ecology

We drop in the evening like dew
upon the ground and the living
feel it on their faces. Death
soft, moist everywhere upon us,
soon to cover the living
as they drop. This explains
the ocean and the sun.

Communion I

To say what has to be said here,
one must literally take off one's clothes.
That I will do.
        Now that I am naked,

you have seen these nipples,
this navel and these thighs
and black beard of my manhood.
All this, you will admit,
is not unexpected. I am
of my own kind
and my heart beats.
I have brothers.

How Else

It's this way: the tree has to be pruned
and watered. Do it yourself.
Then turn to the sun.
How else,
when the hired stranger is a lover
too.

At Four O'Clock

At four o'clock I went by
and she was lying there.
At nine, I found her there again
and on my way home finally
past midnight.
Her face wedged between the iron gate
and the stone stair lay pressed flat
against the stone, a drunk and ill
from afternoon till night
in the dress of an ordinary woman.

Communion II

Let us be friends, said Walt,
and buildings sprang up
quick as corn and people
were born into them, stock
brokers, admen, lawyers and doctors
and they contended
                      among themselves
that they might know
                      each other.

Let us be friends, said Walt.
We are one and occasionally two
of which the one is made
and cemeteries were laid out
miles in all directions
to fill the plots with the old
and young, dead of murder, disease,
rape, hatred, heartbreak and insanity
to make way for the new
and the cemeteries spread over the land
their white scab monuments.

Let us be friends, said Walt, and the graves
were opened and coffins laid on top
of one another for lack of space.
It was then the gravediggers slit
their throats, being alone in the world,
not a friend to bury.

The Outlaw

They went after him with a long stick,
jabbing into the hole where he had hid himself
in its dark. If he could be forced out
they would shoot him. The stick dug
into his soft parts but he lay there.

It poked hard and he moved aside.
They would fire into the hole
but that it would seem it was they
who had something to worry about.
The woods darkened and they left.
He came slowly from hiding
and in the silence sat up to lift his voice,
to those beyond the woods about to go to bed,
mournful and prolonged.
For that he was despised.

Pricing

The grave needed a stone marker.
We picked Flint Rock from New England,
four feet high and three feet wide,
to cover two bodies lying side by side,
my mother and eventually my father.
He stood examining it with us,
his son and two sons-in-law,
in the marble store, and made no comment
other than the weary, grim look
of an old man who has lost his wife,
his only companion, and himself soon to go,
alone now, living among strangers,
though they were his kin.
An old man shuts himself off.
Later after the purchase, as I drove the car,
he tried to say something
to convey his mood and failed,
saying something hackneyed, conscious of it,
and said nothing further, until at home
finally with his daughter he discussed
the price and the stone's color

Business

There is no money in breathing.
What a shame I can't peddle my breath
for something else—like what?
I wish I knew but surely
besides keeping me alive
breathing doesn't give enough
of a return.

Adonis

I am in love with a pig,
she dances for me
on her hind legs. Good pig,
you must love me
and grateful as I'll be
do not turn savage like a boar,
I might find excuse
to keep you alive,
your tusk buried
in my side.

The Rockets

For those who'll take my place,
I'll leave this peace I devised:
I called upon the quiet air
of summer and I sat
in the grassy field and examined the daisy.
It had made itself without suffering
to others and had found itself
a place without the use of force
or displacement of others.
Reclining on the grass on one elbow,
I rose up and walked within range
of the guns and the rockets

In the Woods

My beard rough as the beginning
of things, I'm new today.
You won't find me,
I'll be in the woods
growing a skin
to make friends
with the squirrels, the fox
and the puma; you won't catch me,
I'll be hidden behind their furry selves
and making my own sounds.
Look for me in the trees
or on the mountains,
if you can get away.

The Taste

Let the bombs hang in air a moment
while we adjust to their coming,
making ourselves secure in our will
to die as we are, unrepentant
but forgiving, since we cannot
go on breathing except as we are.
Therefore to be remembered
as we were by the bone pickers
who know the taste of flesh.

Reading at Night

What have I learned that can keep me
from the simple fact of my dying?
None of the ideas I read stay
with me for long. I find the dark
closed in about me as I close
the book and I hurry to open it

again to let its light shine
on my face.

In Ancient Times

And they took Abu and stoked the fire with him,
and then Azu, after Abu was consumed,
to keep the blaze high. It was a night
of wild animals, a fire was needed to ward them off.
Abu by his own choice was killed for fuel
and then Azu to keep the others safe;
and so on down the line, one by one,
until morning. Men, women and children
who would not die in this manner
were forced to by their own hand,
for the sake of the others,
after a long talk.

And in the morning
the great band arose from around the dead ash
and moved on to new grounds and new possibilities;
and in the afternoon as always
when they were starved paired off
and killed each other for their food.
There was nothing to eat over the whole wide plain
of their wandering, and nothing to work with
to turn the soil—like lead, anyhow.
They had come by a blind route from orchards
and fields in their wandering to this
forsakenness, over which the lions howled
for the flesh that crawled by.

Mystique

No man has seen the third hand
that stems from the center,
near the heart. Let either
the right or the left prepare
a dish for the mouth,   ·
or a thing to give,
and the third hand deftly
and unseen will change the object
of our hunger or of our giving.

Bothering Me at Last

Where is my mother?
Has she gone to the store for food,
or is she in the cellar shoveling coal
into the furnace to keep the house warm?
Or is she on her knees scrubbing the floor?
I thought I saw her in bed
holding a hand to her heart, her mouth open.
"I can't breathe, son. Take me to a hospital."
I looked for her in the cellar.

I looked for her in bed, and found her in her coffin,
bothering me at last.

Promenade

His head split in four parts,
he walks down the street—pleasant
with shady trees and a sun softened
by leaves touching it. He walks,
a revolving turret for a head,
from each slit of which he looks guardedly:
the enemy approaches or he approaches
the enemy. At any moment the chatter of differences

will break out; the four parts of his skull
revolve slowly, seeking the time.

In there they do not know of each other,
sealed off by steel walls. They are safer
together, singly and apart;
while overhead, ignored in the walk,
are the leaves, touching each other and the sun.

News Report

At two a.m. a thing, jumping out of a manhole,
the cover flying, raced down the street,
emitting wild shrieks of merriment and lust.
Women on their way from work, chorus girls
or actresses, were accosted with huge leers
and made to run; all either brought down
from behind by its flying weight, whereat
it attacked blindly, or leaping ahead,
made them stop and lie down.

Each, hysterical, has described it in her way,
one giving the shaggy fur, the next the shank bone
of a beast, and a third its nature
from which, as it seemed, pus dribbled,
when she saw no more—
                              all taking place
unnoticed until the first report, hours later
when consciousness was regained, and each
from diverse parts of the city has a telltale
sign, the red teeth marks sunk into the thigh
and the smell of a goat clinging tenaciously
through perfume and a bath.

Dilemma

Whatever we do, whether we light
strangers' cigarettes—it may turn out
to be a detective wanting to know who is free
with a light on a lonely street nights—
or whether we turn away and get a knife
planted between our shoulders for our discourtesy;
whatever we do—whether we marry for love
and wake up to find love is a task,
or whether for convenience to find love
must be won over, or we are desperate—
whatever we do; save by dying,
and there too we are caught,
by being planted too close to our parents.

Oedipus Reformed

I will not kill my father,
he must die of admiration.
I will not lay a hand on him,
I will not curse or nag
or make him to explode angrily
so that his mind bursts.
Here is myself realized,
I have everything I ever dreamt,
and I shall attend his funeral,
mourning my lost heart;
for with him goes my impulse.
And then I will raise him in my eyes,
we will be one.
My wife will play my mother
and be kind.

The Gentle Weight Lifter

Every man to his kind of welcome in the world,
some by lifting cement barrels, laboring.
He looks so stupid doing it, we say.
Why not a soft job, pushing a pencil
or racketeering, the numbers game?
As the pattern is rigged, he must
get love and honor by lifting barrels.

It would be good to see a change,
but after barrels he cannot fool with intangibles.
He could with his muscular arm sweep them aside
and snarl the tiny lines
by which he can distinguish love.

He is fixed in his form,
save a hand reach from outside
to pick him up bodily and place him
still making the movements that insure his love,
amidst wonders not yet arrived.

The Fisherwoman

She took from her basket four fishes
and carved each into four slices
and scaled them with her long knife,
this fisherwoman, and wrapped them;
and took four more and worked
in this rhythm through the day,
each action ending on a package
of old newspapers; and when it came
to close, dark coming upon the streets,
she had done one thing, she felt, well,
making one complete day.

Moving Picture

When two take gas
by mutual consent
and the cops come in
when the walls are broken down
and the doctor pays respects
by closing the books
and the neighbors stand about
sniffing and afraid
and the papers run a brief
under a whiskey ad
and the news is read
eating ice cream or a fruit
and the paper is used
to wrap peelings
and the garbage man
dumps the barrel
into the truck
and the paper flares
in the furnace and sinks back
charred and is scooped up
for mud flats and pressed down
by steam rollers for hard ground
and a house on it
for two to enter.

An Illusion

She was saying mad things:
"To hell with the world!
Love is all you need! Go on
and get it! What are you
waiting for!" and she walked,
more like shuffled up the street,
her eyes fixed upon the distance.
People stepped self-consciously

out of her way. Straight up
stood her hair, wild.

What are you waiting for,
snarled from her lips.
It seemed directed to herself
really, to someone inside
with whom she fought.
The shredded hem of her dress
rustled around her.

The Debate

This man brings me stones
out of the ground. These
are eggs, he says, of the Jurassic
age, hardened. They may
be looked upon as eggs.
And taking them in awe
I drop them. They bounce,
one strikes me on the toe,
I wince. These are eggs,
he repeats calmly.
They are stone, I shout.
Stone, stone! They were eggs
in their day and bruise me now.
They are eggs, ossified,
he amends calmly.
And I will not let you
fry them for breakfast,
I answer sweetly,
because they are stone.

For All Friends

Talking together, we advance from loneliness
to where words fall off into space
and send up no echo. Looking down
for instruction, we gaze into the crease
and fold of each other's face.
We are falling, our flesh aged
by life's upward force.
Our words are buried in the falling air.
Deep in the ground,
we will be one with our words,
for earth too falls towards eternity.

Simulacrum

The world is made up of cab drivers,
truck drivers, bus drivers and ministers
of state who discuss whether or not
another war is due among bus, truck
and cabmen of the world; and if not,
for how long peace can be enforced.
Each minister in the dignity of his office
ponders aloud all sides with eclat;
while from the street rises
the all consuming roar of his constituents.

The Reward

They who love me stand in my way
of being taken care of and fondled;
they call on me for help.
I am afraid, after all, that to scream
and rant will be my downfall.
They will see me coming and run,
and I will die of loneliness;
and so you see me either accompanying my wife

on her walks or in my aged father's business,
and no one would know that I am impatient,
least of all my friends who come to me
with their thoughts. I embrace them,
shielding myself with their presence.

I Have Spoken

I conquer the world with a cough,
I reduce it to a sound of rasping.
I have been at grips with it,
feeling its pull, and I have stood still,
perplexed, the words crowding my throat.
Coughing to relieve myself,
I have spoken.

A Reply

My poems no longer are "Beautiful,"
they are hard to live with,
speaking of my coming death.
Preparing myself, I write of dying.
The living, who come from the other end
of the room, shrink from the sound of it,
for beauty is made
and not lamented on.

IV

Poems of the 1960s

How Come?

I'm in New York covered by a layer of soap foam.
The air is dense from the top of skyscrapers
to the sidewalk in every street, avenue
and alley, as far as Babylon on the East,
Dobbs Ferry on the North, Coney Island
on the South and stretching far over
the Atlantic Ocean. I wade
through, breathing by pushing
foam aside. The going is slow,
with just a clearing ahead
by swinging my arms. Others are groping
from all sides, too. We keep moving.
Everything else has happened here
and we've survived: snow storms,
traffic tieups, train breakdowns, bursting
water mains; and now I am writing
with a lump of charcoal stuck between my toes,
switching it from one foot to the other—
this monkey trick learned visiting
with my children at the zoo of a Sunday.
But soap foam filling the air,
the bitter, fatty smell of it . . . How come?
My portable says it extends to San Francisco!
Listen to this, and down to the Mexican border
and as far north as Canada. All the prairies,
the Rocky Mountains, the Great Lakes, Chicago,
the Pacific Coast. No advertising stunt
could do this. The soap has welled out of the ground,
says the portable suddenly. The scientists report
the soil saturated. And now what?
We'll have to start climbing for air,
a crowd forming around the Empire State Building
says the portable. God help the many
who will die of soap foam.

The Errand Boy I

To get quicker through the day
and to bring on night as a blessing,
to lie down in a sleep that is a dream
of completion, he takes up his package
from the floor—he has been ordered
to do so, heavy as it is, his knees weakening
as he walks, one would never know
by his long stride—and carries it
to the other end of the room.

The Dream

Someone approaches to say his life is ruined
and to fall down at your feet
and pound his head upon the sidewalk.
Blood spreads in a puddle.
And you, in a weak voice, plead
with those nearby for help;
your life takes on his desperation.
He keeps pounding his head.
It is you who are fated;
and you fall down beside him.
It is then you are awakened,
the body gone, the blood washed from the ground,
the stores lit up with their goods.

Say Pardon

Say pardon to a bum,
brushing past him.
He could lean back
and spit
and you would have to wipe it off.
How would you explain
that you have insulted

this man's identity,
of his own choosing;
and others could only scratch
their heads and advise you
to move on
and be quiet.
Say pardon
and follow your own will
in the open spaces ahead.

In Limbo

I have a child in limbo
I must bring back.
My experience grows
but there is no wisdom
without a child in the house.

Sunday at the State Hospital

I am sitting across the table
eating my visit sandwich.
The one I brought him stays suspended
near his mouth; his eyes focus
on the table and seem to think,
his shoulders hunched forward.
I chew methodically,
pretending to take him
as a matter of course.
The sandwich tastes mad
and I keep chewing.
My past is sitting in front of me
filled with itself
and trying with almost no success
to bring the present to its mouth.

Walt Whitman in the Civil War Hospitals

Prescient, my hands soothing
their foreheads, by my love
I earn them. In their presence
I am wretched as death. They smile
to me of love. They cheer me
and I smile. These are stones
in the catapulting world;
they fly, bury themselves in flesh,
in a wall, in earth; in midair
break against each other
and are without sound.
I sent them catapulting.
They outflew my voice
towards vacant spaces,
but I have called them farther,
to the stillness beyond,
to death which I have praised.

Be Like Me

I will walk, if I must,
in a crowd, so that I am kind.
I cannot think, as if I had lost
something that love comes from.
I do not even know
to whom I am talking.
I break off and try to revise.
Someone comes by and whispers,
"Be like me."

And Step

I understand myself
in relation to a stone,
flesh and bone.
Shall I bow down

to stone? Mine
is the voice
I hear. I will
stand up to stone.
I will be proud
and fragile, I will
be personable
and step over
stone.

Content

I should be content
to look at a mountain
for what it is
and not as a comment
on my life.

Blessing Myself

I believe in stillness,
I close a door
and surrender myself
to a wall and converse
with it and ask it
to bless me.
The wall is silent.
I speak for it,
blessing myself.

Whistle or Hoot

The bird that sings to itself
is never a lonely or frightened bird;
though if before it were silent,
darting its head for worms

or worrisome matters,
now that it sings to itself
it triumphs, whistle or hoot.

This Is Mortal

The lit room is blinding.
We are moments of the heart.
There is a silence between beats,
no beat for the same blood twice.
We love one another like the motion
of the blood, and there is no outcry,
for this is mortal
in the bright room.

A Semblance

Over your mother's grave
speak a prayer of bafflement,
grasp the hand of the rabbi,
nearest to steady you.
He recites the prayer
for you to follow unsteadily
its meaning. You pray
to the air.

The Rightful One

I heard my son burst out of his room
and shout, he is here, dad. He is here.
I understood and I managed to stand up,
melting within, and walk the hall
between our rooms to meet Him
whom I had neglected in my thoughts;
but not my son who was ill

and had searched for Him.
He had come. I saw Him standing,
his hair long, face exhausted, eyes sad
and knowing, and I bent my knee,
terrified at the reality,
but he restrained me with a hand
and said, I am a sufferer like yourself.
I have come to let you know.
And I arose, my heart swelling, and said,
I have failed and bitterness is in me.
And he replied, And forgiveness too.
Bless your son. And I blessed him
and his face brightened. And the Rightful One
was gone and left a power to feel free.

Self-Centered

I love the only day that I was born,
as if in my oneness I could love another,
and yet I love a day. As of the beginning
I am here, but have come really
from the second day in which a sky was made.
Before everything I was what I do not know,
an absence, a beginning. There has been none
since the start. Therefore to love my only day
is to be set apart,
and this what I do when I am one,
and there is what has been,
at which time I was the beginning.

The Complex

My father's madness is to own himself,
for what he gives is taken. He is
a single son of God. He is mad
to know the loves he owns are for his keeping,

so if he does not love he is without himself,
for God has said, Of love you are a man.
You are yourself, apart from me.
And madly my father seeks his loves,
with whom there is no standing,
for as he would own himself
he is the measuring rod,
and slowly owes himself to God,
giving of himself with forced breath.

POEMS OF THE 1960S FROM *Poems 1934–1969* (1970)

The Journey

I am looking for a past
I can rely on
in order to look to death
with equanimity.
What was given me:
my mother's largeness
to protect me,
my father's regularity
in coming home from work
at night, his opening the door
silently and smiling,
pleased to be back
and the lights on
in all the rooms
through which I could run
freely or sit at ease
at table and do my homework
undisturbed: love arranged
as order directed at the next day.
Going to bed was a journey.

A Loose Gown

I wear my life loosely around me,
feeling it at elbows and knees.
Sometimes I'm forced to hurry
and it races along with me,
taking the wind in its hollows.
I get out of breath
and would fall down exhausted
but the wind in these pockets
of my life keep me from falling.

Leaping from Ambush

A man goes by with a woman.
Another man cleaning his car
by the curb glances at her
and follows with his eyes
but returns to wiping his car
with a chamois cloth.
                              Is it
the chamois cloth that stops him
from killing the man and leaping
upon the woman?

Love Poem for the Forty-Second Street Library

With my eyes turned to the sky
and my toes nearly touching pavement,
floating along I'll approach Times Square,
the cabs coming to a screeching halt,
whistles blowing and crowds on four corners
huddled together and staring,
my legs trailing above the ground,
my eyes lifted entranced
to the top of the Empire State Building
as they stare unbelievingly,

attaché cases and handbags weighing
them down, their backs aching.
I'll turn my shimmering gaze towards the Library,
my love for it spreading to the crowds
which will begin to sway softly and sing
to themselves of better days that have passed
and been forgotten. Children once with eyes
for everything, now their eyes on the dollar
which too hovers in front of them.

I'll glide up Fifth Avenue, my eyes focused
longingly on Central Park, on perhaps one small corner
where I will lie down and meditate,
and no crowds but each of us
spread in his favorite spot of lawn
or nearby shrub. I'll be followed
like the Holy Grail and later
go to jail for stopping traffic.
I'll turn my eyes upwards to the ceiling.
The warden and his wards will look
upwards with me in curiosity.

Oh judge, I'll plead, my toes trailing
the courtroom floor, I've been happy
this way, my eyes shimmering and turned
upwards.

Where Nothing Is Hidden

Now I understand myself running back
to the city, out of breath and happy
to have escaped the sight of green vomit
and the groaning power lawn mower—
this advertised peace. I wanted
truly undisguised faces of boredom
swirling around me in the street
and my own grim hail to traffic jams,
to death by cops' cross fire,
to dope addiction,

to married life in Brooklyn overlooking the cemeteries
and to the crumbling beer-can-littered schoolyards
of Harlem.
Nothing is hidden.
Nobody lies or covers up.
A low gas cloud covers the city
on which the people slowly choke in bed
but not one's own green vomit to walk on
in silence. It hangs a curtain from the trees.

Scream and yell and pound on the walls here in the city,
to be ignored or beaten down.
Speak of the bitter with your last breath
and sweep the whole city into the sea
with a gesture or drive your car off the dock,
taking with you the city's death,
but none of the green vomit
of those who spill their guts
and stand on it in silence like trees
that hide their birds from one another
and live for hundreds of years
without comment.

Off to the Cemetery

To die is to be brought down among blacks
and Puerto Ricans who live in rat buildings
and inject themselves to endure
the wastes of newsprint in the street.
To die is to be abandoned to the Sanitation
Department that comes to remove you
quickly in an oblong garbage box,
the men ashamed of their uniforms.

The funeral is attended with studied
preparations for a wedding. The event
grows happy and relieved as it concludes
and the body is removed from the chapel.
Then all get to file out. The ceremony

was not to see the departed off
to an eternal rest, life transitory
if blessed, but for a pact, a vow
of renewed heat, life married to death
and made one, and away the guests go
to the cemetery in cars and cabs
that are as good-looking as false teeth.

A First on TV

For Walter Cronkite

This is the twentieth century,
you are there, preparing to skin
a human being alive. Your part
will be to remain calm
and to participate with the flayer
in his work as you follow his hand,
the slow, delicate way with the knife
between the skin and flesh,
and see the red meat emerge.
Tiny rivulets of blood will flow
from the naked flesh and over the hands
of the flayer. Your eyes will waver
and turn away but turn back to witness
the unprecedented, the incredible,
for you are there
and your part will be to remain calm.

You will smash at the screen
with your fist and try to reach
this program on the phone, like a madman
gripping it by the neck
as it were the neck of the flayer
and you will scream into the receiver,
"Get me Station ZXY at once, at once,
do you hear!" But your part
will be to remain calm.

For My Daughter

When I die choose a star
and name it after me
that you may know
I have not abandoned
or forgotten you.
You were such a star to me,
following you through birth
and childhood, my hand
in your hand.
                When I die
choose a star and name it
after me so that I may shine
down on you, until you join
me in darkness and silence
together.

My Place

I have a place to come to.
It's my place. I come to it
morning, noon and night
and it is there. I expect it
to be there whether or not
it expects me—my place
where I start from and go
towards so that I know
where I am going and what
I am going from, making me
firm in my direction.

I am good to talk to,
you feel in my speech
a location, an expectation
and all said to me in reply
is to reinforce this feeling
because all said is towards

my place and the speaker
too grows his
from which he speaks to mine
having located himself
through my place.

I Sleep

I sleep so that in the silence
I can more clearly understand
myself. In darkness
I grope to the center
of my pulsation and find
to my dismay
a beating heart.

FROM *Figures of the Human* (1964)

To an Apple

You were rotten
and I sliced you into pieces
looking for a wholesome part,
then threw you into the street.
You were eaten by a horse,
dipping his head to nibble
gently at the skin.
I heard later he became violently ill,
died and was shipped off
to be processed. I think about it
and write of the good in you.

And That Night

A photo is taken of the family
enjoying the sunshine
and that night someone sneaks up
from behind in your flat
as you sit reading the papers
and clobbers you. You never
find out why or who, you just
lean back and die.
The sunshine is gone too,
the photograph gets into the news.
You bring up a family in three small rooms,
this crazy man comes along
to finish it off.

Play Again

(Late in 1962 New York newspapers reported the story of a nine-year-old child being raped on a roof, and hurled twenty stories to the ground.)

I draw near to the roof's edge
and seek someone to lift
and hurl me out into vacant air.
I want to turn over and over
rapidly in my plunge, my mouth
open to scream but air rushing
upwards jams my throat.
I am seeking the peace
I never once gave up on
and this is the final way
to find it. The living
share me among them. They taste
me on the ground, they taste me
in the air descending. They taste
me screaming, nine years old.
I have playmates

and I leave behind my skull
in their dreams, hands to mouths.
It is because they have no help,
as if to hint to them the way,
if they would understand.
When we played it was to love each other
in games. Play again and love me
until I really die, when you are old
on a flight of stairs.

Earth Hard

Earth hard to my heels
bear me up like a child
standing on its mother's belly.
I am a surprised guest to the air.

The Years of Loss

I love the beginning, always a promise.
I love the middle period
when all are committed
and I love the years of climax
when the beginning is possessed
in the face and the years of loss
in evidence.

In a Dream I

Out of a crowd he steps
towards the iron gate
surrounding the fountain
and recites to himself
between the bars
two lines of a poem

newly arrived—
two lines that he repeats
again and again
until in that talkative crowd
several turn to stare
and say, It's his life he leads,
and look away.

Figures of the Human

My love, pills in her purse,
runs, now staggering, now flushed,
her speech racing near the world:
whisper talk to it, dangling,
"Let creatures ride her, soften hard bumps
for them." Who warns her from self,
racing, singing, lightfooted?
Birds, dogs, cats screech, bark, mew,
conversant with air.
                        Raise her from swooning,
the childhood spirit. Catch her
skittering, mewing with joy, barking delirium.
Then are we loved, hand drawing swiftly
figures of the human struggling awake.

And the Same Words

I like rust on a nail,
fog on a mountain.
Clouds hide stars,
rooms have doors,
eyes close,
and the same words
that began love
end it
with changed emphasis.

The Sky Is Blue

Put things in their place,
my mother shouts. I am looking
out the window, my plastic soldier
at my feet. The sky is blue
and empty. In it floats
the roof across the street.
What place, I ask her.

The Song

The song is to emptiness.
One may come and go
without a ripple. You see it
among fish in the sea,
in the woods among the silent
running animals, in a plane
overhead, gone; man
bowling or collecting coins,
writing about it.

Two Friends

I have something to tell you.

I'm listening.

I'm dying.

I'm sorry to hear.

I'm growing old.

It's terrible.

It is, I thought you should know.

Of course and I'm sorry. Keep in touch.

I will and you too.

And let know what's new.

Certainly, though it can't be much.

And stay well.

And you too.

And go slow.

And you too.

No Theory

No theory will stand up to a chicken's guts
being cleaned out, a hand rammed up
to pull out the wriggling entrails,
the green bile and the bloody liver;
no theory that does not grow sick
at the odor escaping.

For One Moment

You take the dollar
and hand it to the fellow beside you
who turns and gives it to the next one
down the line. The world being round,
you stand waiting, smoking and lifting
a cup of coffee to your lips, talking
of seasonal weather and hinting
at problems. The dollar returns,
the coffee spills to the ground
in your hurry. You have the money

in one hand, a cup in the other,
a cigarette in your mouth,
and for one moment have forgotten
what it is you have to do,
your hair grey, your legs weakened
from long standing.

About Money

The wonder of cherries
has gone into the wonder of money.
My mind is green with anxiety
about money.

Simultaneously

Simultaneously, five thousand miles apart,
two telephone poles, shaking and roaring
and hissing gas, rose from their emplacements
straight up, leveled off and headed
for each other's land, alerted radar
and ground defense, passed each other
in midair, escorted by worried planes,
and plunged into each other's place,
steaming and silent and standing straight,
sprouting leaves.

Prologue

Mine was the life planned to go wrong
and to make havoc among the living.
From me you know what is monstrous
about being alive,
and to forgive myself
and go on eating
I must act like you.

I get up sick inside,
I lie down unlearnt
and in my sleep
hear a wishful tide
cleaning, cleaning.

I was born of parents who had small comfort
for one another. When they met
it was to recognize their need for contrast
and it turned out
they rubbed each other the wrong way.

So when you find out your father
spends his days looking at lewd photos,
you yourself feel so happy and relieved.
Your stomach quakes, your head thick
with whispers, your legs trembling.

Epitaph

There were no hidden motives to his life,
he is remembered for his meanness.
Beyond that we may look into the sky
and lose ourselves in the blue air.

Reason with me,
I'll believe in reason
though my father is dead,
and when I die
remember of me
I sought for a reason.

In the mirror the face I see
before me is my father's face,
as if I were thinking his thoughts
about me, in love
and disapproval.
I turn my face away.

Forgive me, father,
as I have forgiven you
my sins.

Self-Employed

For Harvey Shapiro

I stand and listen, head bowed,
to my inner complaint.
Persons passing by think
I am searching for a lost coin.
You're fired, I yell inside
after an especially bad episode.
I'm letting you go without notice
or terminal pay. You just lost
another chance to make good.
But then I watch myself standing at the exit,
depressed and about to leave,
and wave myself back in wearily,
for who else could I get in my place
to do the job in dark, airless conditions?

Envoi

Strange judgment upon me:
I once said to my father,
You are not my father,
and I meant Karl Marx, Lenin, Whitman.
Today I have a son
to whom I am tempted to say,
You are not my son,
in the same passionate vindication
of myself.

The Bagel

I stopped to pick up the bagel
rolling away in the wind,
annoyed with myself
for having dropped it
as it were a portent.
Faster and faster it rolled,
with me running after it
bent low, gritting my teeth,
and I found myself doubled over
and rolling down the street
head over heels, one complete somersault
after another like a bagel
and strangely happy with myself.

Rescue the Dead

Finally, to forgo love is to kiss a leaf,
is to let rain fall nakedly upon your head,
is to respect fire,
is to study man's eyes and his gestures
as he talks,
is to set bread upon the table
and a knife discreetly by,

is to pass through crowds
like a crowd of oneself.
Not to love is to live.

To love is to be led away
into a forest where the secret grave
is dug, singing, praising darkness
under the trees.

To live is to sign your name,
is to ignore the dead,
is to carry a wallet
and shake hands.

To love is to be a fish.
My boat wallows in the sea.
You who are free,
rescue the dead.

Notes for a Lecture

I will teach you to become American, my students:
take a turn at being enigmatic, to yourselves especially.
You work at a job and write poetry at night.
You write about working. Married,
you write about love.

I speak of kisses and mean quarrels,
the kiss brings the quarrel to mind,
of differences for their own sakes.

Did I ever think, going to bed,
a woman beside me would be no more uplifting
than a five-dollar raise? Since then
I've been uplifted in bed a hundred times
and but once raised in pay,
and that once has not been forgotten.

Take a broken whiskey bottle,
set it on top of your head
and dance. You have a costume,
you have meaning.

Sediment

You are such a well-rounded sponge
from head to foot
that I have made myself a lake for you
not to see you shrivel up
and I have surrounded you with trees
and a distant view of a mountain,
calm sky above.
No rain comes while you and I float together,
your reflection in me, and then slowly
you settle down, filled.
I think you are going to drown
and I will go dry, utterly absorbed in you,
my mud and rock showing. I worry about us,
you swollen and out of shape
and I tasting of sediment.

For Your Fear

Love me and I'll think about it
and perhaps love you,
if it goes with the moment
or in despite of that pose as lover
to find the truth of what to love.
Hate me for that matter
for being so plain
and I will have to think
and keep open between us lines
which might someday carry messages

when it's with you as with me.
Love me for my desperation
that I may love you for your fear.

Ritual One

As I enter the theatre the play is going on.
I hear the father say to the son on stage,
You've taken the motor apart.
The son replies, The roof is leaking.
The father retorts, The tire is flat.
Tiptoeing down the aisle, I find my seat,
edge my way in across a dozen kneecaps
as I tremble for my sanity.
I have heard doomed voices calling on god the electrode.
Sure enough, as I start to sit
a scream rises from beneath me.
It is one of the players.
If I come down, I'll break his neck,
caught between the seat and the backrest.
Now the audience and the players on stage,
their heads turned towards me, are waiting
for the sound of the break. Must I?
Those in my aisle nod slowly, reading my mind,
their eyes fixed on me, and I understand
that each has done the same.
Must I kill this man as the price of my admission
to this play? His screams continue loud and long.
I am at a loss as to what to do,
I panic, I freeze.

My training has been to eat the flesh of pig.
I might even have been able to slit a throat.
As a child I witnessed the dead chickens
over a barrel of sawdust absorbing their blood.
I then brought them in a bag to my father
who sold them across his counter. Liking him,
I learned to like people and enjoy their company too,

which of course brought me to this play.
But how angry I become.
Now everybody is shouting at me to sit down,
sit down or I'll be thrown out.
The father and son have stepped off stage
and come striding down the aisle side by side.
They reach me, grab me by the shoulder
and force me down. I scream, I scream,
as if to cover the sound of the neck breaking.

All through the play I scream
and am invited on stage to take a bow.
I lose my senses and kick the actors in the teeth.

There is more laughter
and the actors acknowledge my performance with a bow.
How should I understand this?
Is it to say that if I machine-gun the theatre
from left to right they will respond with applause
that would only gradually diminish with each death?
I wonder then whether logically I should kill myself
too out of admiration. A question indeed,
as I return to my seat and observe a new act
of children playfully aiming their kicks
at each other's groins.

From a Dream

I'm on a stair going down.
I must get to a landing
where I can order food
and relax with a newspaper.
I should retrace my steps to be sure,
but the stairs above disappear into clouds.
But down is where I want to go,
these stairs were built to lead somewhere
and I would find out.
As I keep walking,

ever more slowly,
I leave notes such as this on the steps.
There must be an end to them
and I will get to it,
just as did the builders,
if only I were sure now
that these stairs were built
by human hands.

East Bronx

In the street two children sharpen
knives against the curb.
Parents leaning out the window above
gaze and think and smoke
and duck back into the house
to sit on the toilet seat
with locked door to read
of the happiness of two tortoises
on an island in the Pacific—
always alone and always
the sun shining.

I See a Truck

I see a truck mowing down a parade,
people getting up after to follow,
dragging a leg. On a corner
a cop stands idly swinging his club,
the sidewalks jammed with mothers
and baby carriages. No one screams
or speaks. From the tail end
of the truck a priest and a rabbi intone
their prayers, a jazz band bringing up
the rear, surrounded by dancers and lovers.
A bell rings and a paymaster drives through,
his wagon filled with pay envelopes

he hands out, even to those lying dead
or fornicating on the ground.
It is a holiday called
"Working for a Living."

All Quiet

> For Robert Bly
> Written at the start of one of our bombing pauses over Vietnam

How come nobody is being bombed today?
I want to know, being a citizen
of this country and a family man.
You can't take my fate in your hands,
without informing me.
I can blow up a bomb or crush a skull—
whoever started this peace
without advising me
through a news leak
at which I could have voiced a protest,
running my whole family off a cliff

For Medgar Evers

They're afraid of me
because I remind them of the ground.
The harder they step on me
the closer I am pressed to earth,
and hard, hard they step,
growing more frightened
and vicious.
                Will I live?   .
They will lie in the earth
buried in me
and above them a tree will grow
for shade.

On the Death of Winston Churchill

Now should great men die
in turn one by one
to keep the mind solemn
and ordained,
the living attend in dark clothes
and with tender weariness
and crowds at television sets
and newsstands wait
as each man's death sustains a peace.
The great gone, the people
one by one
offer to die.

The Signal

How can I regret my life
when I find the blue-green traffic light
on the corner delightful against the red brick
of my house. It is when the signal turns red
that I lose interest. At night
I am content to watch the blue-green
come on again against the dark
and I do not torture myself
with my shortcomings.

Against the Evidence

As I reach to close each book
lying open on my desk, it leaps up
to snap at my fingers. My legs
won't hold me, I must sit down.
My fingers pain me
where the thick leaves snapped together
at my touch.

All my life
I've held books in my hands
like children, carefully turning
their pages and straightening out
their creases. I use books
almost apologetically. I believe
I often think their thoughts for them.
Reading, I never know where theirs leave off
and mine begin. I am so much alone
in the world, I can observe the stars
or study the breeze, I can count the steps
on a stair on the way up or down,
and I can look at another human being
and get a smile, knowing
it is for the sake of politeness.
Nothing must be said of estrangement
among the human race and yet
nothing is said at all
because of that.
But no book will help either.
I stroke my desk,
its wood so smooth, so patient and still.
I set a typewriter on its surface
and begin to type
to tell myself my troubles.
Against the evidence, I live by choice.

An Omen

I love the bird that appears
each day at my window.
Whether the bird loves me
I only can surmise
from its regularity.

An Ontology

In the dark I step out of bed
and approaching the kitchen down the foyer
run my hand over the wall, smooth and rough
by turns, with cracks, holes, lumps
and dips the whole length,
my hand forming to each.
The floor bumpy and creaking,
now straight and now sagging,
the soles of my feet shape to each change.
My shoulders compress to the narrow hallway
as they go forward with me to the kitchen,
and there my eyes blink at the light.
Because I can find no direction of my own,
I eat. I belong with the bread, the milk
and the cheese. I become their peace.
I am nourished with myself
and go back to bed. I become the mattress,
I lie upon myself, I close my eyes,
I become sleep. It rolls me over
as I dream. I become a lack of control,
happening simultaneously everywhere.
It is me, I am happening.
As I move all moves with me.
I am this all as it moves
and harm cannot come unless I happen,
but because I exist, I am existence.

Three in Transition

For WCW

I wish I understood the beauty
in leaves falling. To whom
are we beautiful
as we go?

I lie in the field
still, absorbing the stars
and silently throwing off
their presence. Silently
I breathe and die
by turns.

He was ripe
and fell to the ground
from a bough
out where the wind
is free
of the branches

For My Daughter in Reply to a Question

We're not going to die,
we'll find a way.
We'll breathe deeply
and eat carefully.
We'll think always on life.
There'll be no fading for you or for me.
We'll be the first
and we'll not laugh at ourselves ever
and your children will be my grandchildren.
Nothing will have changed
except by addition.
There'll never be another as you
and never another as I.
No one ever will confuse you
nor confuse me with another.
We will not be forgotten and passed over
and buried under the births and deaths to come.

The Hope

In the woods as the trees fade in the dusk
I am unable to speak or to gesture.
I lie down to warm myself against the ground.
If I live through the night
I will be a species
related to the tree
and the cold dark.

Walk There

For Marianne Moore

The way through the woods is past trees,
touching grass, bark, stone, water and mud;
into the night of the trees, beneath
their damp cold, stumbling on roots,
discovering no trail, trudging
and smelling pine, cypress and musk.
A rabbit leaps across my path,
and something big rustles in the bush.
Stand still, eye the nearest tree
for climbing. Subside in fear
in continued silence. Walk.
See the sky splattered with leaves.
Ahead, is that too the sky
or a clearing?
Walk there.

Brief Cases

It was then that carrying brief cases
was prohibited in public as a mark
of impotence; no man need disgrace himself,
not recognizing his own shortcomings,
obvious to others, especially police
who carried their nightsticks
in their hands.
           "What are men if not men,"
was the motto they wore on their caps
in red and white, with scarves twirled
around their throats, of any color
for their pride. And the women,
oh the women, were unhappy.

It was then that carrying brief cases
in public was prohibited to them too,
for in these brief cases were tiny men
packed neatly in small cartons
to be opened in private homes.
Oh the little men danced on the tables
and kissed the lips of the women
who gave their lips to be kissed,
and the tall men who carried the brief cases
withdrew into the dark rooms of the houses.

Oh the women were not happy
but the tiny men grew tall
and all brief cases were abolished
and replaced by beds
that were then carried on the strong backs
of the tall men who once were little.
Oh the women were not happy,
nor the tall men with all the little habits
of the past.
           How did it all end?

I'm hard put to tell you but I did hear
that the women chose to live
and the once little men and those
withdrawn into the dark
gave birth.

First Coffin Poem

I love you, my plain pine box,
because you also are a bench,
with the lid down. Can you see
my friends in a row seated
at ease with themselves?
I am in a coffin
and it has been set against the wall
of a living room. It is just before
dinner and several friends are standing
about with glasses in their hands,
drinking to the possibilities
that life offers.
                    The coffin also
could be placed as a table
in front of a grand sofa, with food
and drinks served on it, and an ashtray.

It would be so much simpler, less gruesome
to use an actual coffee table, you say,
or a real bench, but ah, that would prove
how rigid we must be about ourselves
and cause us to languish, caught
in a limitation. We must make one thing
do for another.

                    I am hope, in urging you
to use my pine box. Take me to your home
when I die imperceptibly. Without fuss
place me against the wall in my coffin,
a conversation piece, an affirmation of change.
I am, sincerely, yours.

While I Live

I dream of language as the sun.
I whisper to that plant
whose own language is the wind.
It cups its flower to listen
at the wind's pressure and we talk
together of the darkness in language:
what Dante suffered at its command—
only that I may endure the necessary
ecstasy of my personal death.

I want my trees to love me
and my grass to reach up to the porch
where I am no one but the end of time,
as I stand waiting for renewal in my brain,
because I am what the sun shines forth:
I am labor, I am a disposition to live.
Who dies? Only the sun
but you must wait
while I live.

V

Poems
of the
1970s

Invocation

Dirt and stone, if I may know you as you know yourselves,
if you do have sense of yourselves,
I walk upon and study you as my next brothers and sisters,
in this only way I know how to think about you.
I pick you up in my hands and run you slowly through my fingers,
I feel so close to you, if only not to fear
but to know and make you my kin, even if I must do it alone.

I am resigned, if I must say it that way.
Try as I might, I cannot think myself exactly that.
I see us each in separate worlds
and because I must join yours and gradually become as you,
I want to know what home will be like there.

If I could say that from you can be made men and women,
how happy and relieved I'd be to know
we have a sort of exchange program between us,
in which we spring up out of the dust
and are greeted with open arms to tell that all is well
back there growing its fruits.
And then to embrace, all of us together,
and celebrate with drink and dancing
and to see one into the soil
with solemn benedictions on a current of joy,
waving him farewell as he disintegrates to dust.

I speak to you in pity for myself; speak to me
and return the love I must have for you,
since I must be buried one day in you
and would go toward love again, as in life.
Let us be reconciled to one another.
Dirt and stone into which my flesh will turn,
this much we have in common. As I cannot speak to my bones
nor my blood nor my own flesh, why then must I speak?

What says I must speak if I am not answered?
What then that I should speak or am I speaking at all,
if my own flesh and bones cannot answer me,
as if already they were partners of the stones and dirt?

Reading the Headlines

I have a burial ground in me where I place the bodies
without fuss or emotion, hundreds of thousands at a glance.
I stow them in and as it happens I am eating dinner.
I continue to eat, feeding myself and the dead.

I walk around in this burial ground, examining it
with curiosity, find it dark but stroll with a sense
of safety, my own place. I want to lie down in it,
dissatisfied with it, true, but seeing no exit, I lie
down to rest and dream.

I am lost anyway, without horizon or recognizable features.
It's just to walk on. At least it's not necessary
to kill myself. I'll die of attrition of my energy to live.

I know my direction and have companions, after all.

My Enemies

I know how I have learned to hate. I've turned on trees and animals
and crushed the ant in my path. Many a time I've ignored the sun
and the moon in my walk to keep my eyes turned down toward the
dirt of the path or its concrete and often refused to wash my body of
its sweat and oils. I saw no purpose in a tree growing or in the food
set before me. I could see no commerce between men and me. Did
the stars touch each other? Did they reach out to give light when the
light failed in another? Was the sun sympathetic? Did the moon care?
Did my feet warn me of the creatures beneath their soles as I walked?
Who held me in such regard as to want to unburden me of my faults
and let me live? It was a concert of divisiveness without any particular

foe or intention: a salad of kinds of separateness on which I was fed, and because I lived I wondered about all this and remarked on my living. Why, I asked myself, was it not possible to name the faults and hold them as a keepsake for the living? I did this and I survived my pain and everything about the sun was granted for what it was and everything about my parents and my brothers, my food and the soles of my shoes and the separateness of stars and the purpose lacking in the trees and my own divisiveness. Granting all this and knowing that I had brought my own death closer by living this day I thought of such a thing as love to describe it.

I greet the hair on my head, chest and pubic region each morning as my companions in living. I expose my teeth to welcome them in my mouth, teeth that stay with me out of loyalty or their own desire to remain and be. I am prepared now for loving the day. I can be hurt and I brood.

I may take my quiet revenge but hurt and brooding and revenge absorb me more deeply in this meaning, that my life loves my toenails even as I love my enemies.

The Diner

For Sartre

If I order a sandwich and get a plate of ham and eggs instead, has communication broken down? Is there a chef in the house? There's no chef. I get only silence. Who brought me the ham and eggs? I was sitting at the counter when it arrived. I don't remember anyone bringing it. I'm leaving right now to find another place to eat in, a bit more congenial than this silence, with no one to witness that I ordered exactly what I say I did. But now the door is closed and I can't leave.

Will someone please open the door, the one who gave me the ham and eggs instead of a sandwich? If I'm dissatisfied and want to leave why must I stay? Can the proprietor do as he pleases with anyone on his property? Am I his property too? What do you know! I have to eat what's given me or go hungry. I have to be nice about it too and say thank you to the silence. But I want to know why I can't have what I want that's such an innocent wish as between a sandwich and a plate of ham and eggs? What have I said or did I say what I thought I did or am I in my own country where my language is spoken? Where am I? Why can't I leave this diner? This is not my country. I don't belong here. I never even got a passport to come. I don't remember leaving. I don't remember crossing the border and I'm the only guy here at the counter. Something phony is going on. Somebody is trying to drive me nuts or rob me or kill me. I want to go back where I came from. I was on the road hungry, driving. It was dark and I hadn't eaten my dinner.

You know, it's quite possible I made these ham and eggs myself instead of a sandwich. It may be I'm the owner because no one else is here and I have the key to open the door, exactly like my car key. I must have arranged it that way. Now when in hell did I buy this diner and who needs it!

Information

This tree has two million and seventy-five thousand leaves. Perhaps I missed a leaf or two but I do feel triumphant at having persisted in counting by hand branch by branch and marked down on paper with pencil each total. Adding them up was a pleasure I could understand; I did something on my own that was not dependent on others, and to count leaves is not less meaningful than to count the stars, as astronomers are always doing. They want the facts to be sure they have them all. It would help them to know whether the world is finite. I discovered one tree that is finite. I must try counting the hairs on my head, and you too. We could swap information.

Talking to Myself

About my being a poet, the trees certainly haven't expressed an interest, standing at a distance. I'd expect that at least they'd try to learn something new besides growing their leaves, old stuff by now, and anyway it's done by so many others. Wouldn't these trees want to know what they'll be doing in a hundred years, what they look like now, how they stand, what's their name, where they are and what they actually do in winter and in summer, deaf, dumb and happy as they are? Not happy, simply willing to go on as always. Not even willing, just doing what comes naturally. To them I might as well be dead or a tree.

To stay among the trees as if I were at home, arrived from a long journey, I am digging a place for a burial with my feet.

The Weather

Live for myself
said the wind
Live for myself
said the rain
Live for myself
said the night
I bent my head
turned up my collar

My Poetry Is for the Night

My poetry is for the night
of empty buses. I write,
depleted, and hug my death.
Live for others, I hear whispered,
for the child growing,
face of a rushing stream.

I fall asleep
as it were a poem
being written
to resolve my cares
into a final solution
and as my eyes close

and silence spreads itself
inside me like a wave
I know I am succeeding,
and in sleep rejoice.

He Moves

He moves straight before him, legs moving lightly
over ground. Encounters a lamppost
with caressing hands, moves on
to meet a water hydrant he lightly vaults,
eyes lifted to the tall buildings
irregular in height. Smiling as if amused
in sleep he climbs rapidly up one wall.
Tenants sip their coffee and look down
into the street or from the window talk
to someone in the room. He nears the very top
of one skyscraper, lifts a window and steps in
and strides to the other end of the room
and through its wall. Around him conversation
never stops, an office of whirring typewriters.
In the corridor, emerging from the wall,
as he turns to an exit marked by a red light
he meets her on the stairs.

                              They come together,
fuse, her breast becomes his left chest,
his lower lip rouged, right arm muscular,
the left soft, round and exposed at the shoulder,
right hip shaped like a female's
and on his left foot a black high-heeled pump,
his right leg covered by a half skirt.
Still he is smiling but even more broadly
as in sleep. In the hallway where he stands
transformed people rush by to and from
elevators opening and closing.

He explodes.

Each Day

Cynthia Matz, with my finger in your cunt
and you sliding back and forth on it,
protesting at the late hour and tiredness
and me with kidneys straining to capacity
with piss I had no chance to release
all night, we got up from the park bench
and walked you home. I left you
at the door. You said something
despairing about taking a chance
and settling on me. I had left Janette
to chase after you running out
of the ice cream parlor where
the three of us had sat—I had felt
so sorry and so guilty to have you
find me with her in the street.
You and I had gone to shows together.
You needed me to talk to and I was glad.
The talk always was about him
whom you still loved. He had jilted
you for someone else. I'm sorry, Cynthia,
that it had to end this way between us too.
I did not return the next day,
after leaving you at the door.
I did not return the following day either.
I went with Janette in whom I felt
nothing standing in the way,
while with you it would have been
each day to listen to your sadness
at having been betrayed by him.
I was not to be trusted either.
I too wanted love pure and simple.

A Moral Tale

All this for me, he asked,
looking down on her body.
Uh huh, she said, arms stretched out
upon the bed, and she looked up at him
with an amused smile. I think
I'll take it, he said,
and wrapped it up in the sheet
that lay beneath her. He brought
the four ends together in a knot
and slung the body across his back.
He was on his way home to show
his latest find. He had discovered
each body was different
and that altogether they amounted
to a survey of the female form,
something an anthropologist could appreciate,
and he was thinking of becoming one
but there was a hitch: he was bringing
back more bodies than with place
to store them in the house
and it was expensive elsewhere.
He persisted.
He went broke;
his wife left him.
He had to give up his studies;
he had to go back to work
and was left with memories
which to relieve himself in his unhappiness
he would relate at work
where in amazement he was urged to write them down.
The manuscript was published.
The book sold.
There was money again
to return to his studies.

Moral: In adversity we find our goal in life.

Once There Was a Woman Smiled at Me

Once there was a woman smiled at me
from her open door. I wanted her
at once and sat through a political
meeting in her house, thinking
of just this.

At This Moment

I'm very pleased to be a body. Can there be someone without a body?
As you hold mine I feel firmly assured that bodies are the right thing
and I think all life is a body. I'm happy about trees, grass and water,
especially with the sun shining on it. I slip into it, a summer pleasure.

I have hurt the body. That's when I know I need it most in its whole
condition. If I could prove it to you by giving pain you would agree
but I prefer you with your body pressed to mine as if to say it is how
we know. Think, when two must separate how sad it is for each then
having to find another way to affirm their bodies. Knock one against
another or tree or rock and there's your pain. Now we have our arms
filled with each other. Could we not grow old in this posture and be
buried as one body which others would do for us tenderly?

Peace

Peace belongs with the birds,
buffeted by wind,
driven close to the wave's lash.
They have found a place
for storms in their brain;
utter no protest,
their wings widespread.

The Refuse Man

I'm going to pull my stinking wagon
through the streets and countryside,
letting it smell up the highways
and its odor crawl into the one-
and two-family houses along the road
and over the corn and wheat fields
and let the cows raise their heads
from munching to bellow their anger
and the cop to draw up alongside
my wagon—I'll be pulling it
between the shafts—and let this cop,
holding his nose, come over to ask
in an awed voice what the hell
it is I'm hauling and I'll tell him,
as sweetly as I can, "A dish of rotted guts,
an empty skull, a fetid breast, a swarming
belly, a corpse, a man right out
of his mother's belly given his occupation,
and I've put myself between the shafts—
a horse will not come near this;
I had to, being a man."

With My Back

With my back to the insane world
of the next room I look into my poetry
for the gentleness in making do
with the known facts. On his side
of the wall sits a young man
spilling fear from his mouth.
I read in my poetry that fear teaches
me to love and that love also
is the beginning of fear
so that I find myself upon a cutting edge.
He in the room next door is bloody.
I look in my poetry for what to do

to help and read I must remain
absolutely still. He must be allowed
to think he is alone and that the world
waits on him for decision.

The Future

I am going to leave a child in an empty room.
She will have my body to look down on
at my death, when she will ask of the room
its address, the room silent,
stretching across the sky.
What comfort for her, my only expectation,
as in her infancy she climbs upon my lap?

My daughter, as I recede into the past,
I give you this
worth more than money,
more than a tip on the market:
keep strong;
prepare to live without me
as I am prepared.

Autumn II

For Wendell Berry

A leaf lies shaking
at my door, about to be
blown away.
            If I should
bring it into the still
air of my room, it would
lie quietly on the window sill
facing the tree
from which it fell.

For John Berryman

You're dead, what can I do for you?
I am not unsympathetic;
I thought about you often enough
though we never spoke together
but once when I shied away,
feeling something that I fought
in me too—and came out with this
manner of living, by living.

It is depressing to live
but to kill myself in protest
is to assume there is something
to life withheld from me, yet
who withholds it? Think about it.
What is the answer?

But suicide is not so wrong
for one who thought and prayed
his way toward it. I wish, though,
I had known sooner, to have
helped you go on living,
as I do, half a suicide;
the need defended by the other half
that thinks to live in that knowledge
is praiseworthy.

Prose Poem in Six Parts

1

I'm so happy, he shouts, as he puts a bullet through his head. It leaves
a clean hole on either side of the skull, no blood pouring out. I'm so
happy, he shouts at his triumph. He knew it would happen this way,
pulling the trigger. He knew it, he had imagined it and he collapses
of a spasm of joy.

His friends look closely at the clean hole on either side and decide to take their own thoughts seriously too and act. It will not be with a pistol but with each other whom they have had on their minds for so long without daring to speak openly about it. They speak and become transfixed in each other's image. They are not exactly dead, they are unmoving but fulfilled. They are not even aware of being happy or depressed and the way domestic animals roam among them nibbling at their fingers, ears, toes and nose is how these animals eat at flowers and grass. To the transfixed it is a happy identification. They can believe the world is whole, all this without saying a word, their eyes starry.

2

Their eyes starry, their bodies glistening with sweat that acts like a lacquer to seal their pores, they grow rigid, gleam like polished stone. They can recall the one who put a bullet through his head. He has risen and walks among them tapping on each body for a response to his happiness, each tap like his heartbeat to inform each rigid body exhibiting its own happiness. These are mutually dependent acts but tapping his way from body to body, his imagination proven to him, he is not aware of their happiness while the one person who is aware of this dilemma has not yet shot himself in the head or talked to another human about each other. He could be lonely were it not for the sight of these who are so happy in themselves. They promise much and he has a relative hope for the future.

3

He has a relative hope for the future. He lights up a cigar and observes the community of polished stones and the one pierced skull and wishes to make himself totally familiar with their lives. He examines the clean hole in the head. He treats himself to a glass of wine. He has doubts, he finds it hard to discover their sources. By examining himself in the mirror he can see his mood. By turning his face from the mirror he can see the bath. By turning from the bath he can see the towel rack. By turning from the towel rack he can see the toilet bowl. By turning from the toilet bowl he has made a complete circle and is back staring into the mirror. It's somebody about whom he has doubts, he has discovered in one complete revolution. By marching out of the bathroom he will leave the image behind him in the mirror and by leaving it behind he is free. Who is he now? He has doubts.

4

He has doubts. He chews upon the stump of his cigar. He can express himself but to what end? Language is not the solution. He can join the rigid aggregate community but in what posture? He could make love to himself but with what thoughts? He could warm himself by the fire in winter, cool himself in the sea in summer. He could eat when hungry. He could cry when in pain, he could laugh when amused, he could think when in trouble. He is an ordinary man.

5

He is an ordinary man, he wants his breakfast, he needs his unhappiness, he wishes to be himself, he desires apotheosis as he is and so he shoots himself to relieve himself of his doubts. Brought to consciousness by this act, he dies. The man with the clean hole through his skull does not know the ordinary man is dead and the aggregate community never cares to change from its transfixed postures while he, lying dead, is studying that compelling emptiness in him beneath his breastbone and does not know how either to fill it or extract it to give him peace. He yearns to leap up from the floor to become a whirling dancer, an ecstatic, for the hell of it.

6

For the hell of it he tries but lies still. He then knows he is dead and would inform the world. His body will, he decides. It is the evidence and his silence the message, and now what does life have to offer? It is time to think. He thinks, the earth has the answer that it presses upon him where he lies. Not to think is the answer. He can be a stone or a cycle of existence, inside the cycle the air of emptiness, a small hole for a small life such as he had seen in the skull of the risen one. He can be a stone with a hole in it and he will always be the same. He has his comfort, he is ready to die successfully, he dies and is complete, an ordinary man.

I Shake My Fist at a Tree

I shake my fist at a tree
and say, You will shed your leaves
in time for all your abundance
and variety but I will see to it
that you continue in your present
state in my mind. You have no
memory except in me. I'm
about to write of you
leaf by leaf.

Those dead brown leaves lying at my door
as if to let me see them in their last condition
before they disappear into the fields, I am
your only witness. If I live to have
to see you dead, then there is no answer
to your death but life, and I am living it.

Going Down

There's a hole in the earth I'm afraid of.
I lower myself into it, first tying
one end of a long rope to a tree close by,
the other end around my waist.
I let myself down hand over hand,
gripping the rope hard,
with each step planting my feet
solidly against the sides
that give off an earth odor.

As I descend I breathe less of air
and more a mingling of minerals and clay,
wet, heavy, close. I begin to lose
consciousness and I am afraid
I will loosen my grip on the rope
and fall to the bottom and be suffocated

by dirt chunks falling on top of me
from off the walls. It was this
fear of burial led me to climb down.

Melpomene in Manhattan

As she walked she would look back
over her shoulder and trip
upon sidewalk cracks or bump
into people to whom she would apologize
profusely, her head still turned.
One could hear her murmur to herself
tearfully, as though filled with a yearning
to recover what she was leaving behind
as if she would preserve it
or do for it what she had neglected
out of ignorance or oversight
or from sheer meanness and spite
or simple helplessness to do better,
her voice beginning to keen
as she tripped or steered blindly
into the gutter
or into hostile crowds.

Their Mouths Full

Let there be ripeness, said the Lord.
And men bowed down to seed brown in the pod
and to its meat palpable and sweet.
And of this fruit you shall eat
for your wisdom, said the Lord.
And of none other, lest you die.
And the men ate of the ripened fruit
and rejoiced in its taste
and of the seed split between their teeth,
for these too were sweet of their kind;
and so it happened that unripened fruit

was looked on with scorn
and beaten down from its branches
in the Lord's name as sinful
and the work of death.
And men sat themselves down to grow
palpable and sweet to one another
in the sun and it was then time to die,
ripening, and they died,
blessing their maker,
their mouths full of one another.

In a Dream

at fifty I approach myself,
eighteen years of age,
seated despondently on the concrete steps
of my father's house,
wishing to be gone from there
into my own life,
and I tell my young self,
Nothing will turn out right,
you'll want to avenge yourself,
on those close to you especially,
and they will want to die
of shock and grief. You will fall
to pleading and tears of self-pity,
filled with yourself, a passionate stranger.
My eighteen-year-old self stands up
from the concrete steps and says,
Go to hell,
and I walk off.

Thinking

I am caught in the body of a fish.
If I am the fish itself this speech
is the sound of water escaping
through my gills and like all fish
I will be caught in the mouth
of a larger one or be netted
or die of being fish. Thinking
that I am caught inside, a person
with a right to freedom as I've been
trained to think, my thought is another
kind of net because this right
to freedom is a torment like being
caught in the body of a fish.

With Others

When I see fish swimming in schools,
I'm very sad
that we must stay apart
in this only world we have
between us. I see looks exchanged
among men and women, lips to bodies,
and when they part, I think
I am surrounded by a loud wailing
in the air. I raise my voice
in grief too, my one identity
with others.

Brightness as a Poignant Light

I tread the dark and my steps are silent.
I am alone and feel a ghostly joy—wildly
free and yet I do not live absolutely
and forever, but my ghostly joy
is that I am come to light
for some reason known only to the dark,
perhaps to view itself in me.

As I tread the dark,
led by the light of my pulsating mind,
I am faithful to myself: my child.
Still, how can I be happy
to have been born only to return
to my father, the dark, to feel his power
and die?

I take comfort that I am
my father, speaking as a child
against my fatherhood. This
is the silence I hear my heart
beating in, but
not for me.

From the Observatory

Each step is to and from an object
and does not echo in heaven
or in hell. The earth vibrates
under the heel or from impact
of a stone. Many stones fall
from outer space and earth itself

is in flight. It heads out
among the stars that are dead,
dying or afire.

The Seasons

The seasons doubt themselves and give way
to one another. The day is doubtful of itself,
as is the night; they come, look around, slowly depart.
The sun will never be the same.
People give birth to people, flourish
and then die
and the sun is a flame of doubt
warming to our bodies.

With the Sun's Fire

Are you a horror to yourself?
Do you have eyes peering at you
from within at the back of your skull
as you manage to stay calm, knowing
you are being watched by a stranger?

Be well, I am seated beside you,
planning a day's work. We are contending
with the stuff of stones and stars,
with water, air, with dirt, with food
and with the sun's fire.

Examine me, I am continuous

Examine me, I am continuous
from my first memory and have no memory
of birth. Therefore was I never born
and always have been? As told

in my breathing which is never new
or tired?

        Face in the mirror
or star hidden by the sun's rays,
you are always there but which am I
and who is the mirror or the hidden star?
Explain me as you are that I may live
in time and die
when I am dead.

The Two Selves

I existed before my mind realized me
and when I became known to myself
it was with the affection for warmth
beside a radiator.

        So you began for me
and I will whisper to your self
to give in, to surrender, to close
in remembrance, and I will give you up
and withdraw into a stone, forever
known to you.

The Juggler

He bows and extracts from his pockets a live rabbit, a tiger cub, a
rooster, a monkey, a musical instrument. Is it an oboe? And he is
ready and heaves all into the air with one heave and quickly catches
each one on its way down, then sends them up again, singly this time,
one after the other. They squawk, hiss, growl, chatter, crow. The oboe
emits music! In protest? Who can tell? It is music and that's all. And
the juggler is laughing, laughing like a clown and nobody wonders
why he uses things alive.

Scenario

An old man realizes that he is seeing signs of a bodily reversion to his youth. His skin appears fresh and smooth around the thighs where it had been wrinkled and flabby; his white hair shows streaks of the original black, his sagging chin line is gone. One morning, he confronts the startling image of himself in his twenties. It frightens him and exhilarates him also, and he goes rushing to show himself to his wife who looks at him and begins to weep.

He grows younger still and leaves his wife and finds himself a young woman to live with. Life is merry again, and he grows younger still, and his new wife begins to laugh at him. He has regressed to his teens, mind and body reverting to an excitable, incoherent stage. He grows even younger, becomes a lisping child, becomes an infant, then a squalling newborn. He returns to fetus stage. He loses all sense of himself and his surroundings. He becomes an ovum. For all practical purposes, he no longer exists, but when he begins to sense himself again it's as he emerges from a wet, pulsating warm cleft with the help of a pair of forceps around his throbbing head.

Paint a Wall

Paint a wall
cover the weather stains
and spider webs: who's happy

You who don't exist
I make you
out of my great need
There is no prose for this
no ordered syntax
no carefully measured tread
I am falling beyond depth
into oblivion
breathing
I hear breathing

Something must be said
of nothing

I am as queer as the conception of God
I am the god and the heaven
unless I scatter myself
among the animals and furniture of earth

An Account in the Present Tense
of How It All Happened

I am about to close the refrigerator after removing a package of meat
when I hear my door lock turning and a crew of men, without so
much as first knocking, walk in. They stride directly over to the refrig-
erator, tie rope around it, hoist it upon a dolly and ride it out the door.
Who are these people and why are they taking my refrigerator when
there is nothing wrong with it? They are making some kind of mis-
take. Stop, I cry. You are in the wrong apartment. Not one turns his
head to look at me or to listen. At that moment, three men, a second
crew almost on the heels of the first, stride in and lift up my television
set between them and walk out with it. I scream for help. I pound
their shoulders but get no response, as if they were made of wood. I
scream and scream, and another crew is right behind the second, this
time to remove my bed. I am going to be left with nothing, nothing.
I am about to get on the phone to call the police when I notice that
they have cut the wires and taken the phone with them.

They remove dishes, cutlery, rugs, books, lamps; screw out the bulbs.
They leave me an empty apartment and begin to tear down the apart-
ment walls. They knock out the walls of the building itself. I flee into
the street, just barely in time before they begin to attack the stairs
and the elevator. Out in the street I see that it's happening to each
apartment building on the block. All the tenants are milling around,
with the few clothes on their backs they managed to grab, and are
shouting at each other in panic and wild rage. We are totally stranded;
there are no police and no emergency crews in sight. The streets are
beginning to resemble a bombed-out area, and we see that we will

have to fend for ourselves with our bare hands. There is a park nearby, and we begin to converge upon it. It has large, open spaces where we will be able to lie down and rest and perhaps make our beds there for the night with what linen and bedclothes we were able to rescue from inhuman hands. It's all over, it seems, that which gave us our comforts and pleasures. It's back to the woods and fields. Did anybody bring a knife or a gun with which to hunt a rabbit or a bird? We look at each other, beginning to understand.

Midnight

It's midnight, the house silent,
in the distance a musical instrument
being played softly. I am alone.
It's as if the world has come to an end
on a low musical note.

Blue

The sky makes no sense to me.
What is it saying? Blue? That blue is enough?
The blue of emptiness?

A small cloud trails beneath the sky
as if to make a point
about its pride in being a body,
white, welcome to the eye.

The cloud drifts out of sight.
In its absence, I will walk
beneath the sky, slowly drifting
in and out of streets and bars.

Scissors

I hold a pair of scissors over my head and open and close the blades to cut off the air from its source. I lower the scissors to the ground and snap at the surface to punish it for its errors, such as grass, trees, flowers and fruit. I turn the scissors' point toward myself, snap the blades open and shut at my nose, my eyes, my mouth, my ears. I have to be angry at myself also who lives off earth and air.

Why is there hurt and sorrow? Scissors, cut them off from me. Scissors, whose fine steel gleams in the sunlight like a most joyful smile, why am I not like you instead, since I must give pain? I do not want to feel it in others. I do not want to feel it in myself. I do not want to be a man cutting through grass and flesh in the sunlight.

Apocrypha

People came to watch him
chew on steak or pear
and spit it out. He
sat cross-legged or moved about
silently, shaking hands
mildly or patting a shoulder,
speaking always in low, pleasant tones.

What was to be made of this man
who did not eat, drink or defecate
in the world? He seemed
to want only to taste its fruits
and let them go, happy
that the world had so many
wonderful flavors. It was this
that irritated observers, and many
hated him, after secretly trying
his way, and starving, shrunk
to skin and bones. It proved
to them he was not human,
and so he died.

Death of a Lawn Mower

It died in its sleep,
dreaming of grass,
its knives silent and still,
dreaming too, its handlebars
a stern, abbreviated cross
in tall weeds. Where is he
whom it served so well?
Its work has come to nothing,
the dead keep to themselves.

Who Could Have Believed It?

Who could have believed it? This is hell and I am looking out upon
grass and trees. The air is calm, it's the beginning of Spring and soon
leaves will sprout and give us a green hell and a warm sun and lake
to swim in to cool us off, then to dress and dine towards an evening
film of the hell of others, which surely we will enjoy for its art and in
private admit it should be lived, since living has no other form for us.
Rise up from your seats, Ladies and gentlemen, and turn in for bed,
locking your bodies together to affirm yourselves.

The Life They Lead

I wonder whether two trees standing side by side really need each
other. How then did they spring up so close together? Look how their
branches touch and sway in each other's path. Notice how at the very
top, though, they keep the space between them clear, which is to say
that each still does its thinking but there is the sun that warms them
together.

Do their roots entangle down there? Do they compete for nourish-
ment in that fixed space they have to share between them, and if so, is
it reflected in their stance toward one another, both standing straight
and tall, touching only with their branches. Neither tree leans toward
or away from the other. It could be a social device to keep decorum

between them in public. Perhaps their culture requires it and perhaps also this touching of branches to further deceive their friends and associates as to the relationship between them—while what goes on beneath the surface is dreadful, indeed, roots gnarled and twisted or cut off from their source by the other and shrunken into lifelessness, with new roots flung out desperately in a direction from the entanglement, seeking their own private, independent sources. As these two trees stand together, they present to the eye a picture of benign harmony, and that may be so, with both dedicated to the life they lead.

The Question

I dream I am flying above the city
on the strength of my two outflung arms
and looking down upon the streets
where people are like so many
bacteria moving about upon a slide.
I am alone up here, with no one
to contradict me, free of the noise,
tumult and violence of the living.
Here is my true residence,
and if I say the people are bacteria
who will deny it? I declare
in my circumstances that the people
are what I say they are. The only
question now is whether I can
keep flying.

I Sink Back Upon the Ground, Expecting to Die

I sink back upon the ground, expecting to die. A voice speaks out of my ear, You are not going to die, you are being changed into a zebra. You will have black and white stripes up and down your back and you will love people as you do not now. That is why you will be changed into a zebra that people will tame and exhibit in a zoo. You will be a favorite among children and you will love the children in return

whom you do not love now. Zoo keepers will make a pet of you be-
cause of your round, sad eyes and musical bray, and you will love
your keeper as you do not now. All is well, then, I tell myself silently,
listening to the voice in my ear speak to me of my future. And what
will happen to you, voice in my ear, I ask silently, and the answer
comes at once: I will be your gentle, musical bray that will help you
as a zebra all your days. I will mediate between the world and you,
and I will learn to love you as a zebra whom I did not love as a human
being.

The Vase

See how tall and straight I stand
with blossoms above me. Could anything
be more beautiful than I who am nothing
but an enclosure upon emptiness?

The Metamorphosis

Bumping against rock in the dark,
he becomes the rock, stiffening in pain.
The pain fades and he becomes the lightness
and relief. He moves
and becomes the movement.
A rock in his path once more,
he falls to his knees
in awe of his past self.

His knees make him a suppliant
of his changes. He seeks to know
and becomes a form of the curious.
He touches himself at all points
and becomes his hands.
They touch stone,
a change he remembers,

and he becomes the remembrance
and moves nimbly in the dark
from rock to rock.

Hair

Did you know that hair is flying around in the universe? Hair trimmed from beards in barbershops, from mustaches at the mirror, from underarms, from crotches, legs and chests—human hair. It all gets dumped into a fill-in space and then the wind gets at it and sails it back into the cities and towns and villages, right through your open windows during summer and even during winter down your chimney. Hair, brown, black, red, white, grey and yellow. They get all mixed up and you find them on your pullover sweater and wonder who did you come up against with yellow hair which you happen to like and you dream of its actually having happened that you were in touch with a person with yellow hair.

That's not the whole of it. Think of walking through the street on a windy day or even on a calm, balmy day. The hair is floating all around you and you are walking through perhaps an invisible or fine mist of cut hairs. Black, brown, red that you would not have cared to touch in a million years because you associate them with certain kinds of faces and behavior but there are the hairs of these people touching and clinging to you, as if trying to tell you that hair is everywhere and everybody has it and that it's hopeless to try to pick black or brown or red off your sleeves but not yellow hair.

It would be an act of insanity. You need to pick them all off or none and let yourself be covered by them all, like a new kind of fur coat or perhaps a new hairy skin to protect you from the weather. Hair of all colors. What a pretty sight that would make, wouldn't it, and you would have a coat of many colors, and I bet you would be proud of it, especially if you saw everyone else wearing a coat of many colors. How about that? Because people cut their hair and let it fly out over the world where it lands on everyone and everyone is sharing in the coat of many colors.

I Live Admiring the Sky

I live admiring the sky
and the mountains and loving
the day and the night, so glad
they are with me, my eyes open,
my nostrils breathing air,
my feet beside the lake,
the sea sound of my heart's beating
at anchor up and down
in the slow swell,
my life oceanic
reaching into the distance.

I Am Brother

I am brother to the tree,
runner with the rabbit
who twitches his ears in the silence.
I cannot figure my own cost,
not in money, no more than I can count
the wind that wraps me around.
On my death the world will go broke.
In me will have been poured its treasure.
The sun, desolated, will stand empty
as the wind.

I Want to Be Buried

I want to be buried
under the angel of a tree
among the cherubim of grass
and lion of the wind
softly in my ear
and lamb of the rain.
I am gone.

Time has happened to me,
minute hand on face of the earth.
Earth is a happiness of its own
as running water
as flowing grass
as the flight of birds.

In This Dream I Do Not Exist

In this dream I do not exist. This I know since it is my dream. How have I come to that conclusion when it is I who dream it? No one else thinks I do not exist but no one has enquired because no one knows I am dreaming. Therefore, since to myself I do not exist, it is true simply because I say so. This, then, is the problem: when I cease to dream will I exist or not exist?

I would like to become nothing for the pleasure of the great leap beyond being that becoming nothing alone can achieve. I can become nothing because I am something and I am something because it can lead to nothing. Can I ask of my life more than that it bring me to its transcendence, that I should be in search of it, as the work of being itself?

My dream, then, of not existing is my being telling me where I must go and what I must welcome as the rounding out of my completeness. I say this in the best of health and in expectation of a long life.

Lightly

To look for meaning is as foolish as to find it.
What does one make of a sea shell
of such and such color and shape,
an ear or a trumpet, rose and grey?
It has been spat upon the shore
out of the sea's mouth. Is this what we mean
by our thinking? This, in wonder? So

that thought itself must pause,
holding the shell lightly,
letting it go lightly.

I'm a Depressed Poem

You are reading me now and thanks. I know I feel a bit better and if you will stay with me a little longer, perhaps take me home with you and introduce me to your friends, I could be delighted and change my tone. I lie in a desk drawer, hardly ever getting out to see the light and be held. It makes me feel so futile for having given birth to myself in anticipation. I miss a social life. I know I made myself for that. It was the start of me.

I'm grateful that you let me talk as much as this. You probably understand, from experience; gone through something like it yourself which may be why you hold me this long. I've made you thoughtful and sad and now there are two of us. I think it's fun.

Hello

A prominent poet receives a national award for the perfect form of his poems.

Hello, drug addict, can you become a poem of perfect form?
Hello, Mafia, can you become a poem of perfect form?
Hello, schizoid person, can you become a poem of perfect form?
Hello, raped girl, can you become a poem of perfect form?
Hello, dead, napalmed man, can you become a poem of perfect
    form?
Hello, incinerated Jew, can you become a poem of perfect form?
If you can't, then you don't deserve to live. You're dead, don't exist;
we want clean earth; get out, get going, get lost.
We have built a house for ourselves called the Perfect Form
and we're trying to live in it, and if you can't take
your napalmed body and your drug-addicted brain

and make them into a poem of perfect form then you don't belong
here. Go somewhere else. Go to Vietnam, where all
the imperfect bodies are and stay there and don't come back
to this country where only the poem of perfect form is wanted.
That's all we live in; you're a foreigner and we don't want you.
You're a kook and we hate you. You're a shit
and we wipe you off the face of the earth.
If you can't make yourself a poem of perfect form
then you have no right to be in this country.
You're here without a passport. You've lost your citizenship
rights. You're an alien, you're a spy.
You're somebody we hate.

Hello, poem of perfect form, we're home again to you
and we're going to snuggle up to you.
You give us so much comfort and pleasure.
We can run our hands over your darling self
and feel every bit of you; it's so sensuous and delicious;
it's so distracting from those bastards outside
who want to disturb us with their imperfect poems.
Fuck me, poem of perfect form.
Let me fuck you. We'll fuck each other.
We have each other, right, so let's do all the nasty
things we dream about and we'll have fun and nobody else
will know about it but you and me and me and me and me and you.
Wow. I don't want to hear another word
except your groans and sighs.

Finally

Finally, I'm sitting here at my desk because I'm afraid to venture into
the street to be accosted by a person asking for help that would mean
my whole life. I have only myself to spare and I need it to help me.
Those who cry out for help have somehow lost themselves, given away
or simply been robbed. I have to stay at my desk to keep myself as I
am, though it's little enough, but it gives me my presence and place
to be.

It is a selfish act, if I can read your thoughts, and I am ashamed, but I am fearful too to act on my impulse to love, the love for others to which I bow my head but refuse to honor because I'm afraid to love beyond myself. I know this, as my heart pounds when I get up to step outside. This is my love, I confess, and I shall remain here to write of it as my acknowledgment, to get it out for others to see and understand. They may knock on my door and ask to be let in. I may let them see me crouched over my typewriter, fearful, showing them my back, but glad that they have come to see me writing of my love, my one way to express it without losing myself in their arms.

Epilogue

The trees are tall gods
commanding a view
of my study. I bow
my head over my typewriter
and start the ceremony
of a prayer.

Inside Me Is the Peace of an Egg

Inside me is the peace of an egg,
round and smooth to myself,
white as a beginning.
Outside my window snow is falling
on the sagging garden shack,
so peaceful too under snow.

Peace of the snow, silence and stillness
where no figure treads.
This is a warm death
under a snow roof.
I want to live amid silence and falling snow.
I want the snow to believe me
and fall peacefully until I fall
from my place in spirals like a flake.

I hear blackbirds breaking the silence.
Keep the newspapers out of the house
and take the phone off the hook
and let the mail rot in the mailbox.
I can't take disturbance, I love the snow.
My life is happier under snow,
I nestle in my own warmth.

It will be days before another human being approaches,
the drifts are too high around the house.
Snow without fault.
I am prepared to enjoy it.

VI

Poems
of the
1980s

My Own House

As I view the leaf, my theme is not the shades of meaning that the mind conveys of it but my desire to make the leaf speak to tell me, Chlorophyll, chlorophyll, breathlessly. I would rejoice with it and, in turn, would reply, Blood, and the leaf would nod. Having spoken to each other, we would find our topics inexhaustible and imagine, as I grow old and the leaf begins to fade and turn brown, the thought of being buried in the ground would become so familiar to me, so thoroughly known through conversation with the leaf, that my walk among the trees after completing this poem would be like entering my own house.

Behind His Eyes

A man, tied to a tree, thinks he is beginning to feel something of the tree enter his body. It is hard for him to discern what it could be, but he would like to grow tiny branches from his head, and leaf buds.

He loves standing still. He thinks he can feel the tree pressing up against him, as if it were trying to instill in him its nature and its seed. He is in a kind of trance about himself. Thinking, as he had sensed before, is no longer a function of thought but of action. That is because he has welcomed the possibility of tiny branches and leaves that now he believes are growing from his sides and from his head. He would laugh in pleasure but that he finds himself swaying back and forth as in a dance that could have been induced by wind.

He is very happy, very much the tree, and he has shed his alarm at having been tied to it in the middle of the woods and left to die. He can forget the reason for his captivity which he thinks of no longer as capture but as a piece of luck to have happened in the midst of this crisis in his life. He is free of crisis, and can celebrate by bringing forth more branches and leaves, and he straightens up from his now stooped posture of exhaustion to let new growth emerge more easily from head and sides. He is alive and that is what counts, alive in a form he has always admired, and now it is his and he is glad, only to find himself growing more sharply stooped and losing memory of himself, as this last thought becomes the bark he has seen behind his eyes.

A Cloud Creates

A cloud creates the face of a man who, happening to look up, recognizes it as his own. The face under stress of the wind begins to disintegrate into wings, and the man sees in himself the ability to fly. He stretches forth his arms and waves them up and down as he begins to circle and dip as a birdman would in the currents of the wind, and then the face vanishes and the wings drift apart, too, in shreds and patches.

The clouds darken, as they will; thunder rolls from their colliding with each other. Lightning flashes. He knows he is at war with himself, the reason for which he cannot go into at the moment.

There is no consolation, not until the rain ceases and the sun emerges and once more clouds arrive, white, brilliantly lit, and so for him full of hope. He has not attempted to sort out his, as it seems, random feelings since sighting the face. And though there is no order to his feelings, of that he is certain, he needs none, not while the sun rises and sets and weather prevails. It is from weather that he derives, and so he has no faults. He is without fault, he is of the weather.

To Oneself

Admit the sky carries no threatening message
in cloud or color. The birds wing by,
your only disturbance and pleasure. The grass
gives you gentleness and the earth selflessness.
You are encouraged on all sides by the impersonal.
Admit: the grasshopper sways upon a blade of grass,
men rest themselves upon the flood.

In No Way

I am of the family of the universe, and with all of us together I do not fear being alone; I can reach out and touch a rock or a hand or dip my feet in water. Always there is some body close by, and when I speak I am answered by a plane's roar or the bird's whistling or the voices of others in conversation far apart from me. When I lie down to sleep, I am in the company of the dark and the stars.

Breathe to me, sheep in the meadow. Sun and moon, my father and my father's brother, kiss me on the brow with your light. My sister, earth, holds me up to be kissed. Sun and moon, I smile at you both and spread my arms in affection and lay myself down at full length for the earth to know I love it too and am never to be separated from it. In no way shall death part us.

Tomorrow

I exist without the dignity of stone
that does not bother that it exists,
and so let me place my hand upon an open flame
and cry out my pain because I exist.
What other is there, without an open hand
into which the apple falls at end of autumn
or that cups the rain of a summer sky
or opens to the sun or moon? I am
the door to tomorrow.

In the Garden

And now I wish to pray and perform
a ritual of my devotion to the sun.
I will bow and sing beneath my breath,
then perform the dance of farewell
and my confidence in the sun's return.

All is dance: the sun glides along the horizon;
now the leaves sway;
now the earth spins.

Of That Fire

Inside I am on fire. Imagine, though, coming up to City Hall and ask-
ing if there is a Department of Burning Need, ready for emergency, I
the emergency. I can see myself being locked up gently in a madhouse
and declared as finished in this world of material evidence. Are my
clothes on fire? Is my hair burning? Are my cheeks aflame? Do my
feet scream with pain? My voice is calm and my clothes intact, my
hair and face moist with sweat, and the oils of my body—normal.
"Where is the fire?" the cops will ask sarcastically, giving me a ticket
for speeding my brain beyond the legal limit and remanding me to
court. I will plead guilty and admit to it publicly, for I'll have no evi-
dence but my spoken word and all the while I'll know that the cop,
the judge and jury too, are burning within, with not a shred of evi-
dence either. They'll laugh and shake their heads and signify with a
twirl of their fingers at their temples a crazed man before them, which
will prove to them how sane are they, not knowing they are dying in
the fire that was lit in them, born of that fire.

I Dream

I dream I am lying in the mud on my back and staring up into the sky.
Which do I prefer, since I have the power to fly into the blue slate of
air? It is summer. I decide quickly that by lying face up I have a view
of the sky I could not get by flying in it, while I'd be missing the mud.

Each Stone

Each stone its shape
each shape its weight
each weight its value
in my garden as I dig them up
for Spring planting,
and I say, lifting one at a time,
There is a joy here
in being able to handle
so many meaningful
differences.

For Yaedi

Looking out the window at the trees
and counting the leaves,
listening to a voice within
that tells me nothing is perfect
so why bother to try, I am thief
of my own time. When I die
I want it to be said that I wasted
hours in feeling absolutely useless
and enjoyed it, sensing my life
more strongly than when I worked at it.
Now I know myself from a stone
or a sledgehammer.

I Identify

I identify with the wooden shed in my neighbor's backyard and with
cords of wood neatly piled. I am identified with the necessary, whether
I myself am necessary. Why does a man go on breathing when he is in
despair? How would it help to know, consciously, clearly, rationally,
but what is rational about the ncessary? If to live and have pride in
oneself is rational, then the necessary is rational. I say to my neighbor,

I hope that you will have a warm fire from those cut logs and that your wooden shed will keep your tools clean and safe from dirt and frost, and I begin to feel myself bodily alive again, proud to have a body like any shed or cord of cut logs.

One Leaf

One leaf left on a branch
and not a sound of sadness
or despair. One leaf left
on a branch and no unhappiness.
One leaf all by itself
in the air and it does not speak
of loneliness or death.
One leaf and it spends itself
in swaying mildly in the breeze.

I Am

I assume a Buddha-like expression in the mirror.
All that is needed now is to remove the doubt
lingering in my eyes, staring back at me
with amusement. It could be the Buddha,
all comprehending, entertained
to see me wish for that
which already should have been.

And so I am not he, nor can ever attain
to his role, but that he could shine
out of my eyes in the mirror tells me
he exists because I wish for that
which, as Buddha, I should have become.

I am, and so Buddha and I are not one,
but this is for my human self
to know he exists and that I exist
in his eyes and am understood.

A Modern Fable

Once upon a time a man stole a wolf from among its pack and said to the wolf, "Stop, you're snapping at my fingers," and the wolf replied, "I'm hungry. What have you got to eat?" And the man replied, "Chopped liver and sour cream." The wolf said, "I'll take sour cream. I remember having it once before at Aunt Millie's. May I bare my teeth in pleasure?" And the man replied, "Of course, if you'll come along quietly," and the wolf asked, "What do you think I am? Just because I like sour cream you expect me to change character?" The man thought about this. After all, what was he doing, stealing a wolf from its kind, as if he were innocent of wrongdoing? And he let the wolf go but later was sorry; he missed talking to the wolf and went in search of it, but the pack kept running away each time he came close. He kept chasing and the pack kept running away. It was a kind of relationship

A Requiem

My father, listening to music, that's me,
my legs outstretched upon the bed
as I lean back in my chair. I think of him
in his chair, legs crossed carelessly
and with his musing smile recalling his first wish,
to become a baritone, his smile seeking
after his youth or watching it in the distant past,
untouchable. I am alone, and the opera playing
heightens my loneliness, without son, without father,
without past or present, and my future a problem.

Eh, father, as I listen to your favorite opera
you would have enjoyed my listening and approved
emphatically, while I'd withhold myself,
tentative towards opera, as other matters burned in me,
such as the need to be free,
and so we would argue but soon fall silent
and go our separate ways.

I am alone in my apartment, alone as you were
without me in your last days at about my age.
I am listening to Rossini and thinking of you
affectionately, longing for your presence once more,
of course to wrestle with your character,
the game once again of independence,
but now, now in good humor
because we already know the outcome,
for I am sixty-six, going on sixty-seven,
and you are forever seventy-two.
We are both old men and soon enough
I'll join you. So why quarrel again,
as if two old men could possibly settle
between them what was impossible
to settle in their early days?

1905

While my father walked through mud
in shoes borrowed from his sister,
all Kiev attended *Prince Igor* and cheered,
and while he worked in a cellar bindery
and slept on workbenches rats leapt over
at night, Dostoevsky's *White Nights*
and *Anna Karenina* were being read avidly
amid joy, tears and protests. My father
was the silent one, walking through the streets
where the hot arguments went on about poverty
and guilt. He walked, his work bundle under arm,
from cellar to monastery, to bind holy books
and volumes of the Russian classics,
and when they had had enough of classics
and needed blood, he fled,
for his blood was real to them; only he
had worked and starved. All others were
but characters in a novel or a play—
bless Chekhov, Gogol and others for their genius,
but my father was the one who had not been

immortalized and made untouchable.
Only he was real in Russia's torment.
Only he stood for life. All else was books,
and that was the torment.

Kaddish

Mother of my birth, for how long were we together
in your love and my adoration of your self?
For the shadow of a moment, as I breathed your pain
and you breathed my suffering. As we knew
of shadows in lit rooms that would swallow the light.

Your face beneath the oxygen tent was alive
but your eyes closed, your breathing hoarse.
Your sleep was with death. I was alone
with you as when I was young
but now only alone, not with you,
to become alone forever, as I was learning
watching you become alone.

Earth now is your mother, as you were mine, my earth,
my sustenance and my strength,
and now without you I turn to your mother
and seek from her that I may meet you again
in rock and stone. Whisper to the stone,
I love you. Whisper to the rock, I found you.
Whisper to the earth, Mother, I have found her,
and I am safe and always have been.

The Ship

I saw an ocean liner in the desert, its crew leaning over the railing,
as though the ship were plowing through the waves of sand. I was
reluctant to ask how a ship came to rest in the desert. The world itself
was strange enough, and I did not want to ask questions that would
make matters worse. I hailed the crew from my position on the sand

and asked where the ship was headed and was answered promptly, Into the desert. I asked to come on board and at once a rope ladder was handed down. I climbed eagerly; we would go through with this absurdity together since, after all, it was our experience, and we could help each other to live it through.

The Bread Itself

Mother, in my unwanted suffering,
I turn to you who knew suffering
like an odor of food and breathed it in
with that familiarity. I can learn
from you to become my self, eating my sorrow
with my bread and gazing frankly at the world
as a man, as you, a woman, taught me
by your silence and acceptance of sorrow,
the bread itself.

Father and Son

A black man is hugging me around the throat from behind with his forearm as he demands in a rapid undertone my money. I think of his embrace as nearly an affectionate one, as if from a son who has come up from behind to demand his stipend for the week in a playful imitation of a mugger. I turn carefully as I would to a son for whom I have the greatest affection and say gently, "The money is in my breast pocket," and I make a motion toward it with my hand. He strikes my hand, as if carrying on the game of mugger, in case, as in the game, I was reaching for a gun. I say again gently to my black son, "The wallet is in my breast pocket." He does not smile. He lets me reach into my jacket to bring forth the wallet, which I do, and he snatches it from me. The game between us has become serious. I am in danger, but I react with calm.

Is this my son, this tall, husky young man who is extracting the bills from the fold and now returning the wallet? I am cautious. I did not train him to be a killer or threatener, but he is serious about the money, and he pockets it all. I have an empty wallet that I return automatically to my breast pocket. He and I look at each other. I think I have a smile on my face, and I think he sees it and is mildly astonished, and maybe understands it or is curious to see a smile. We look at each other for another moment. There is curiosity between us. This is not my son but another man's, and he is acting towards me as a stranger. We are strangers, but we are to each other in the relationship of father and son by age. He opens the door to the elevator and orders me in. Will he kill me in the elevator? I look into his face; he must realize what I am thinking. He holds open the door, waiting for me to enter, not threatening me, simply waiting, and I enter. The door closes behind me. I look through the porthole to see him looking back at me. Is he taking a last look at the man who could be his father whom he has subjugated to his will? I think I am still smiling. I think he is smiling back as the elevator begins to climb.

Above Everything

I wished for death often
but now that I am at its door
I have changed my mind about the world.
It should go on; it is beautiful,
even as a dream, filled with water and seed,
plants and animals, others like myself,
ships and buildings and messages
filling the air—a beauty,
if ever I have seen one.
In the next world, should I remember
this one, I will praise it
above everything.

Thus Truly

The sounds of labor in the street, hammers at work to open pavement, ignore me. Everything is itself and so must return to itself after the event toward which it travels, as does the hammer that strikes at the pavement repeatedly but takes on nothing of its grayness or concrete strength. One resists while the other insists, and there is no meeting of qualities that each could appreciate and want to share.

I am striking at myself to open and plant a tree or make room for my friend who then I could say was a close, loving companion, going with me wherever I must go. This is what it means to be alone.

What keeps me intact after each strike is to know that my face has taken on the shape of each blow, and when I meet with others we measure our suffering at a glance. In deepest secret we are each other's subject of pain, thus truly as one.

Between Shade and Sun

I'm alive to prove the existence of death in me too,
I'm alive to make death visible to myself and to others,
and I think that to be alive with these thoughts
is to be experiencing death at the same time.

I go from one thought to the other as in a walk
from the dark side to the sunlit and back to dark
when the sun grows too hot for my uncovered head—
uncovered in honor of the sun, when as it starts to burn
my scalp I know it is time to move across the street
and into shade. I walk until I tire of the cool,
once more longing for the sun, as I gaze
upon its brilliant pleasure in itself.

I commute between two worlds
and expect to succumb in time to one or the other,
for if I linger in the sun too long
the shade will come upon me from within
and if I walk in shade I will grow cool as death,
but having walked in both shade and sun
I will have lived forever
in seeing nothing change but variations
in the change from shade to sun.

A Discussion

I'm looking for the idea of order.

Where are you looking for it?

Under the table.

How about the closet? Or under the bed? Or in the kitchen sink? Or in your pants pocket? Or in your wallet? Perhaps in your head?

I can't imagine finding it there.

Well, have you looked in the jails?

No, but I have looked in the bars.

How about the grocery stores? How about the banks? Or a garage?

Or a skating rink?

We'll find it, keep looking. You're not doing any harm.

And that's good?

What would you call it?

A kind of order.

An idea in search of its order? I know that in my mind I crave it.

And in my mind I miss it.

That's saying the same thing.

Of course, and I just remembered that there once was a woman with a very hairy face. I remember her from my childhood when I went with my father on a visit. I was struck dumb and all the way home later I could not say a word to my father as I kept thinking of this hairy face.

And that to you was a sign of disorder?

Yes, and I remember on a stroll with my father up the block we lived on passing a jewelry store with a man seated at the window repairing watches. I turned to my father and I said, I am going to become a watchmaker when I grow up. He smiled and said, Yes? And I nodded vigorously.

And that was a sign of order?

Yes.

Do you recall what happened to that hairy lady?

No. She was married to the house painter to whom we had gone to make arrangements to paint our house. He seemed not the least upset by his wife's appearance. And that felt like . . .

Order?

Yes.

So there was both order and disorder in that house?

I don't know whether that actually was the situation and I can't believe it can exist, given the same condition for both in the same place.

Then must we say that we don't know whether there was order or disorder or both?

Right.

And we don't have any solid answer to go on?

We're in the dark.

And all is as if back in a kind of first chaos.

Right.

And we have to live with it.

Right.

And make our peace with it in some kind of order.

A very tentative and problematical kind.

As for your ambition to become a watchmaker, did you become such a person?

It left my mind as soon as I became interested in something else.

And so you lost at least one idea of order through your own thinking and found yourself thinking of another kind of order.

I have forgotten what that one was.

On Freedom

In a dream I'm no longer in love. I breathe deeply this sense of free-dom, and I vow never again to seal myself in, but I am reminded it is myself I love also and that too is a kind of sealed condition. I am com-mitted to taking care of my body and its home accommodations, its clothes and neat appearance that I admire in the mirror, yet I would like to know what it would be like freed of brushing my teeth, washing my neck and face and between my toes. I'd like to know, as I neglect to move my bowels, and stay away from food that could sustain my health, and do not change my underwear, and let odors rise from my crotch and armpit. I stick out my tongue at the image in the mirror showing me my ragged beard and sunken eyes and hollow cheeks, free of my self-love at last, and I sink onto the bathroom floor, feeling life begin to seep out of me, I who haven't eaten since last month. I'm dying and I'm free.

Now I Hear

Now I hear two unsynchronized steel hammers pounding on steel, making contrapuntal sounds between them, as if to teach me the first simple lesson about order, that there are many kinds, and that two could cause discordancy between them as harsh as war; and now one hammer has stopped and it seems as if the other is pounding away even more rapidly to gain on the other if and when it starts again. I sit at my desk waiting for the answer, but now the silence is complete, the second hammer fallen silent, and I am left at my typewriter to make the necessary sounds that we associate with life.

I Saw a Leaf

I saw a leaf flying in the direction opposite the ground, but there was no wind. Now how could that be, I wondered. It was a dead leaf, shriveled and brittle looking, one of the many hundreds that were dropping off the trees upon the ground beside my house. Puzzled for an explanation, thinking that perhaps an updraft had caught the leaf and sailed it into the sky. I watched it grow smaller and smaller to the eye, and soon I could not make it out at all. I shrugged and entered my house and closed the door behind me. I could imagine the house beginning to take off too, and I sat down as if to pin it to the ground, when as I seated myself, there was a tapping on the door. I was expecting company. I approached and opened the door. A single leaf lay on the doorstep at my feet.

With Horace

With Horace I take my stand beside the rocks
and clear falls. I will not be confused
by sound or the stone's hardness. Voices
emerge from me and hardness takes from me
its quality, for Horace lived upon a mountainside
and made shapes that were not pliant.
He dug for rock, as I am, of the born elements
compressed. Did he crush his wine grapes

underfoot? Did he mix with the rain
and the rivers? Who gave him grapes to grow?
Hard money. And am I sick, then, being happy?
He entered a stone house and struck off
his fire upon stone.

FROM *Leaving the Door Open* (1984)

From the Beginning

The sweetness in a man, the very one about to set out to kill a stranger in the forest for poaching his preserves of wild animals, vegetation and fruits: he plays upon his clay pipe melodies about himself: his love for children, wife, tribe and land. It sets others to listen, nod and glance at one another knowingly and to focus on him the more closely to hear how he reaches them in their feelings about themselves and their affections. He gathers spear and sword in his hands and steps softly into the woods to kill. He grinds his teeth in expectation of killing with a fury that will brook no resistance of the creature he is after to make it die in its blood.

Later, he will take up his clay pipe to play in the knowledge that he has killed one that too delighted in the fruit and vegetables of the forest and that loved having been born into its offerings. He will play and perhaps call it a prayer to the mystery of having to live and die in a surrounding of plenty that never in itself will die, as if to dream one could take from it the power in food to live forever but for some baffling reason is never to happen. As he plays, suddenly, because he cannot solve the mystery of his own eventual disappearance, perhaps by the spear of his enemy, if not age—suddenly, in frustration with the question, he will begin to dance, to dance out the disappointment in thinking, in questioning, in searching in himself for an answer. He will dance unto exhaustion, and all who have been listening to him play since the beginning, startled to see him rise to his feet to dance, will join him, his bafflement theirs, as it conveyed itself to them in his playing from the beginning.

Here in Bed

Here in bed behind a brick wall
I can make order and meaning,
but how do I begin? How do I
emerge without panic
to the sounds and mass
of people in the street?

Are they human who stare
as I pass by, as if sizing me up
for a mugging or a filthy proposition,
and am I human to have to be
frightened and on guard?

It's people I'm afraid of, afraid
of my own kind, knowing their angers
and schemes and violent needs, knowing
through knowledge of myself
that I have learned to resist,
but when I can't I have seen
the havoc I have made.

It's this, knowing their desperate motives,
as I have known mine, I'm afraid of
in them. I hide upon a bed
behind a brick wall and listen
to engines roaring up and down
the street and to voices shouting
to one another and find no meaning
or order in them, as there is none
in me when I am free of self-restraint.

The bed is my victory over fear.
The bed returns me to my self
as I was young and dreaming
of the beauty of the trees
and faces of people.

I No Longer Want

I no longer want to feel with you
your tragedy—if but for a moment
to experience death. That cannot
bring home a salary, a toy
for my child, a poem to tell
of my life with or without you.
I will be known for the steadiness
with which I carry grief,
so that one could use me
as a pillar for a house.
And since this tragedy is for us both
you will see me in the distance
walking firmly, so that you
will want to follow,
leaving death behind.

Stranger

Stranger in my life,
I will take care of you
even after my death—to whom
I give the feeling of a father
to his grieving son, for whom
the father will do anything
to make him live.

             Stranger,
the cause of my bitterness
at your condition, and my strange pride,
you my son since no one else
comes to claim you and since I
am sworn to myself to give you all
a father can: love, pity and faith.

Whatever Contribution

Whatever contribution I was to make to living
has been made, yet living has gained nothing
from it but a sharpened sense of its futility
for me. The robin hops from branch to branch
as if one branch makes a difference over the other
and hopping in itself is important to the cause.

Standing idly at the door to the meadow,
not knowing of anyone in need of me,
made unwanted to myself, I glimpse
my neighbor standing in his doorway
too and staring out.

Stability

There is a fault in the universe
that I should have the fault of self-doubt.
The constant exploding outwards
into space, as if to occupy it all
to leave no room for doubt.

If there's no end to space,
then there is no end
to explosiveness, and to racing outward.
With space finite, the universe
will turn in on itself, crushing
each particle of self in search
of assurance, constancy, stability.

The Violence

The language among the clashing winds
and falling trees is action, unexplained
to me or to themselves and unmediated
by feeling for or against—neither

open to discussion with others
nor with themselves. That leaves me
tongue-tied and in a hurry
to secure my safety within
my house, and the trees bend
ominously toward it
beneath the violence of the wind.

No, it's no use longing
for lyric joy, sorrow or fear. It's
no use longing for words of love
or pleading. It's simply to act
as do the trees or the wind:
to become an agent of that force
that could save my life,
and so I become impersonal to myself,
a mind of the wind.

The Bird

The bird was flying toward me
from a distance and as it drew near
to where I stood watching
from behind the deck window
it veered off into the woods
as if I were a stranger
among the grass and flowers.

One bird giving me an insight
into its reasoning
could make me feel at home.

For Now

How the zebra died in the mouth
of the lioness after a brief struggle
of the legs, and then the herd went back
to feeding on the grass nearby
while the lioness and her cubs knelt
at the body as in worship
and ate their fill.

They were soon quiet and resting
on their full bellies and looking
steadily at the herd feeding itself
with heads down to the grass,
not minding the lioness or her cubs.

It was a reassuring sight,
that there was death
and that it had its place
among the living, and a time,
and that time had passed
for now.

Two

The steam hammer pounds with a regularity on steel I should envy.
Neither the hammer nor the steel seems to be suffering from this
terrible meeting between them, proving something vaguely pointed,
that some things must be done, regardless of cost, and finally the cost
too is absorbed in the doing that has become a ritual between two
fated opponents.

The Need

He has come to the conclusion,
walking between the empty lot
and the stone heap, his arms filled,
that this is the life. Stones fall

from his loaded arms and bruise
his feet. He trips. He could
pick flowers, he could heap his arms,
but with stones there is
always the danger,
the need to be alert.

Night

How good it is to feel the joy at last
of oneself. It is like the full moon
shining down upon the dark trees. It is
like lit trains sliding by in the dark.
It is the light of houses in the distance
punctuating the night.

The Men You've Loved

The men you've loved are one man,
the women I've known are one woman;
I hold your hand and look
into your face with love, in peace.
We lie down together
and nothing matters
but making each of us
the first and the last.

Coupling

Wherever he looks, standing still in the city,
are people born of coupling, walking in gray suits
and ties, in long dresses and coiffed hair,
speaking elegantly of themselves and of each other,
forgetting for the moment their origin,
perhaps wishing not to know or to remember.
They dress as if having been born in a clothing store.

They were born of men and women naked
and gyrating from the hips
and with movements up and down
and with climactic yells,
as if losing their lives
in the pleasure and so glad,
so wildly glad.

From this rises the child
from between the wet crotch, blood and mucus.
He stands upright and pronounces himself
humankind and steps from bed and clothes himself
in a gray suit and from the next room of birth
steps a woman in a long dress. They meet
in the corridor and arm in arm walk its length
in search of one room, empty of inhabitants
but prepared for them.

Across the Room

He was caressing the back and shoulders
of the woman seated beside him, his head
turned toward me in conversation, when
this woman started from his caress
and observed quite casually she was not
his wife, who without his knowledge
had changed her seat and was laughing
at him from across the room.

Everyone

Everyone touch everybody's lips. It's ritual, it's important. Now form
a circle, everyone, and look at each other. What do you see? Another
person, naturally, but what else? You see yourself through the eyes of
another. You see yourself as another, and these crosscurrents of sight
meet and would cancel in passing through but are stopped to become
entwined, tense knots of air.

You are not a woman, as the woman opposite looks at you, and you are not about to imagine her a man. You would wish she were one to make things easier between you.

If only you were a woman, she is thinking. How much easier life could be for both, but the knot of air stays tense between you, and you have to smile because there is no other way to ease and dissolve the tension; you are each as you are, so you step forward out of the circle and hold out your hand. She promptly follows with outstretched hand, and to your surprise, it happens with each person in the circle, each holding the hand of another, a hand no different from your own. You could be holding hands with yourself, but the voice speaking to you is another's, and this difference is what interests you to go on being yourself talking and loving.

Meeting

Finally, I have reduced you to a human being.
I have recovered my own humanity,
as you concede quietly. I listen and am sad.
We are two mirrors standing opposite
each other, in one another's reflection.

Where is your first experience
of ruling me with your eyes,
you who must be looking for me
behind my eyes and my reserve
only to find that I am once again
a disappointment, as we are to ourselves.
I am my own small independency
and you the kingdom of yourself.
We meet to form a treaty of respect
and commonality, touching
at the borders of each other's self,
our bodies meeting on a bed.

Lost Childhood

How was it possible, I a father
yet a child of my father? I
grew panicky and thought
of running away but knew
I would be scorned for it
by my father. I stood
and listened to myself
being called Dad.

How ridiculous it sounded,
but in front of me, asking
for attention—how could I,
a child, ignore this child's plea?
I lifted him into my arms
and hugged him as I would have
wanted my father to hug me,
and it was as though satisfying
my own lost childhood.

I Wish a God Were Possible

I wish a god were possible,
at least for me, to find myself
content in that knowledge
and as I die believe an immemorial mind
will hold me in remembrance live
and let to walk about
in an eternal sense of self,
as children do, looking up
into the sky, of which they sense
themselves a part, the sky boundless.
Children think so,
and in my wish for god, I am a child
feeling in myself the wish
that is itself a god
in being boundless.

I've wanted to write my way into paradise

I've wanted to write my way into paradise,
leaving the door open for others. Instead
I am scribbling beneath its walls,
with the door shut.

What is the magic word?
Is there a magic word?
Am I standing beneath the walls of paradise?
Does paradise have walls?

Friends, strangers and relatives look to me
patiently or with sneers and amused tolerance,
crowding around, waiting for the door to open
at my words, but all I can offer are these
questions. They see me uneasy, seated
with my back against the wall,
my eyes closed to rest, to sleep, perhaps
to dream of the paradise
we were to enter at my words.

Without Recrimination

It is wonderful to die amidst the pleasures I have known and so to
die without recrimination towards myself and others, free of guilt at
my shortcomings, happy to have lived and happy to know death, the
last of living, my spirit free to sing as when I felt it born in my youth.
The youth of it returns in dying, moving off from anger that racked its
throat.

With death before me, I look back at my pleasures and they were you
whom I held close in loving, and in the poems I've written for this
truth, which is their beauty and lets me die in pleasure with myself. I
did not fail my life.

In Dream

I died and called for you,
and you came from a distance,
hurrying but impassive. You
looked long and steadily
at my face, then left and strode
back into the distance, rapidly
growing smaller to the eye. You
vanished, but where I lay
I could hear your voice
low and quick, urging me
to awaken to the sunrise
at the window of the bedroom
where we slept together. I
rose up and followed you
into the distance, and there
heard the laughter and wit
with which we had spent
our days together. Then silence,
and I knew we both were dead,
for you had spoken to me
in death, as only the dead
could do, and so at last
we were together.

Concrete

We roll apart, lie side by side,
quiet. We talk of love, family
and troubles. In silence we regard
each other's life and check the time
for school, trains, schedules,
business calls. Getting dressed,
we take our bodies with us

like heavy bags slung
across our backs. Breakfast is food;
words are conversation; lips kissing
good-bye are flesh; cars starting up
to take leave are of metal,
and the road is concrete.

It Is

It is heart-rending to know a kiss
cannot cure the world of its illnesses,
nor can your happiness, nor your tragedy
of being a discrete person, for the bodies
fall like rain into the ground
and merge only to make an ocean
of bones and closed eyes, our identities
merged, as we had wanted
when we were persons
in each other's sight and touch.

The Principle

Make no mistake, you cannot take
my love without accepting my body,
and you cannot accept my body
without a claim to all that I am
and shall always be, that which
has determined me from the beginning,
in the branches of the rain,
in the blood of animals and trees.
As you take me in your arms,
you are making love to all the world
that I am.

The Separate Dead

The leaves on the tree in front of my house—they live and die together, with subtle shades of green at birth and subtle shades of brown and yellow at their deaths. Everybody stands around to admire them and then each goes about his business in separate houses, beds, tables and chairs, with separate knives and forks and living rooms with separate lovers, husbands and wives, and each dies alone, to be buried separately.

The leaves grow thin and wasted-looking, curl up and fall off the branch by the hundreds, like paratroopers from their planes, silently prepared for the next move.

Those leaves that fall upon the graves will lie mouldering and in the rain-soaked earth turn to moss and add their portion to the ground in which the dead are lying, the separate dead.

In My Childhood

In my childhood I awoke to my mother's voice
in the kitchen and knew I was someone
cherished, I belonged. I could look out
the window bravely and admire
the silent, drifting clouds
and look down upon the silent street
and lend my presence to give
its character of trees and sky. Everything
existed in itself in my childhood,
as though between the walls of a synagogue
where I could sit identified as the child
who had yet to learn and was willing.

And when I stepped into the street
among the people walking swiftly past me
to business or to their private affairs,
I shrank from the separateness it made of me.
Now as I lie in the breaking dawn,

frightened of the silence around me,
I am fighting panic that everything
does exist in itself alone.

Wait

I am a man and do not know why I was born. I can tell you the facts:
my mother conceived me when my father lay with her, but that is not
what I'm asking about. Why did they think it was necessary for me
to be born? I can understand love and the desire to have something
to show for it, but should I live on that promise, my parents buried?
For whom now should I live when I am dying, as did my parents who
left nothing of themselves but me who am about to die? If there is
anyone with an answer, let him or her step forward I am patient and
can wait.

I Write

I write to capture the meaningless as it were an animal in the thickets
to hold in my arms; my identity in this animal which, since it exists
for me, gives me my reality too. Whitman, I am happy to say, turned
inside out, having found the answer to his answer, and away I go,
cutting through woods and across fields and rivers back to cities with
a shout of absolute terror. Why? Because here the meaningless exists
too, ready to kill me with a knife or a bullet or a crazy drug. So I shall
be killed, and I will weep in my grave, missing the meaningless.

Trough

I'll watch that mailbox as if it were an ikon of some religious order
about to bring me a blessing from another world. After lunch, I'll sit
back on the sofa which faces the window and look out from time to
time, lifting my eyes from the daily press and, when the mailman ap-
pears and spends the first few moments in sorting out my mail from
the others, my heart will quiver. And when I do open the letters, I'll

find I'm back with people, side by side, as at a trough, eating our way through life out of each other's hands.

The Interview II

I represent *The Morning Shout*. We hear you are dying. May we interview you before you pass on?

Certainly. There won't be another such another opportunity, I'm sure.

We'd like to know what you will miss most, at your death.

Music, nothing but music. Classical and popular, if someone or an orchestra will play during my last hour. I'll be very thankful.

Are you happy to be passing on?

Well, I'm of two minds about it. One, I'd like to hang on a bit longer and, on the other hand, if I can't, I'd like my passing on to be considered an event of some importance.

Next question: Do you have any regrets for having lived as you did? Is there anything you would have done differently if you were given a second chance?

Oh, yes. I'd like to have said hello to my parents more often rather than ignoring them, as I did, even as a young man. I'm sorry about that.

Is there something you can say you are proud of having done in life that you would do over again if given the chance?

Oh, yes. I enjoyed making lots of money, and I'm very proud of having left a fortune. It was a pleasure to accumulate, and I'd gladly do it again, especially to see my name listed in the Obituary, with mention of my wealth. Excuse me, I think I'm beginning to sink rapidly. I will have to say good-by to you for now.

One last question: What are you experiencing at this moment in passing on?

Oh, a slight headache and a feeling of missing out on something. Good-by.

Finally: Are you dead and, if so, can you describe it for us, for your admiring public.

No comment.

The Image

The image in the mirror feels nothing
towards him, though it is his image. He
weeps, and it weeps with him, but is merely
the sign of his weeping, yet he knows
he cannot eat, drink or make love
without that image. He is in awe of it.

Though it does not need him,
he is its servant as he stands there,
doing what is necessary
to keep it in the mirror—humbled
and grateful for its presence,
that which reveals him to himself.
If there is a god, this is he.

VII

POEMS
OF THE
1990s

The World

The world is so difficult to give up,
tied to it by small things,
my eyes noting movement,
color and form. I am watching,
unable to leave, for something
is happening, and so I stand
in a shower of rain
or under a hot sun, worn out
with looking.

The Sunlight, Piercing the Gloom of this House

The sunlight, piercing the gloom of this house,
has pierced me to where memory lives
of a prophetic joy when I was young,
now quiescent, nearly forgotten
beneath the surface of my aging
but for the sudden entrance
of sunlight into this house.

Sometimes I Think I've Lived Too Long

Sometimes I think I've lived too long,
repeating mistakes and pleasures.
What are trees, grass, and sky to me
but emblems of the life that escapes me?
In my search for religion
I have found science;
in my search for final cause
I'm contained in its study.

This Is the Solution

This is the solution: to be happy with slaughter;
to be confident in theft; to be warm and loving
in deception; to be aethetically pleased
with unhappiness and, in agreement,
to lie down in the blood of our innocence.

Here I Am with Mike

For Dan Rather

Here I am, with mike in hand, shooting down the rapids in my business suit, broadcasting to the world my sensations as I near my death. Occasionally you hear me blubber, a wave having knocked against my mouth. But it all gets said, though when I plunge over the falls the force of it will knock the mike out of my hand. In the meantime, I keep my head, reporting myself in fear, fright and elation at the experience I could have only by shortening my life. I'm enjoying it all.

I Killed a Fly

I killed a fly
and laid my weapon next to it
as one lays the weapon of a dead hero
beside his body—the fly
that tried to mount the window
to its top; that was born out of a swamp
to die in a bold effort beyond itself,
and I am the one who brought it to an end.
Tired of the day and with night coming on
I lay my body down beside the fly.

Buzz

Why was I born if I have to die,
buzzed the fly, and buzzed and buzzed,
and when it grew tired it rested.

Permanence

I am leaving earth with little knowledge of it,
without having visited its great cities and lands.
I was here for a moment, it seems, to praise,
and now that I am leaving I am astounded
to have been born at all.

So what does cruelty mean in these circumstances,
and what does triumph, empire and domination,
but waves upon the still sea beneath.
And what does failure mean but to sink below
into the permanence of ocean of our being.

In Me

The leaves of the tree hide the sun
but often enough it shows itself.
Whether it is so intended,
I myself am here by accident.

There is no mercy in things.
There is no warmth in becoming.
Trees, mountains, earth and water
will vanish in me.

Here I Am

Here I am
at the toilet bowl
overlooking the cemetery
and as I gaze down
at my own foregone conclusion
calmly piss.

To Stay Alive

Because words have no effect upon the wind
or the trees, I am a curious onlooker,
but I know that if I were a tree
I too would bend in the wind
and try not to despair. If I were a tree
I would want to believe the wind
had a purpose, because to save myself
would imply to stay rooted
is to stay alive.

His Name

I hear a child singing,
her father dead,
killed in a drunken brawl
with his buddies.
In the street
as she waits for her mother
to take her for a walk
she makes up songs
in which she sings his name.

Shadowing the Ground

What I had witnessed had been lived through
and died of by a young woman in labor
in the house across the street from mine
where I sat at my window and looked out
upon the still curtains of that house,
silent after the first outburst of grief.
I sat, a young man awaiting my own experience,
I would have to leave my room.

Now white-haired,
on that same street

silent
as it had always been,
its trees shadowing the ground,
I have forgotten her name.

The Fish That Lives at the Bottom

The fish that lives at the bottom
has no name. It enjoys the sea
about itself and the dark, knowing
it will never leave and that, when
it ceases to exist, it will exist,
nevertheless, in the anonymity
of the sea.

White-Haired, I Walk in on My Parents

White-haired, I walk in on my parents
and they, in their twenties, dark-haired
and with fresh complexions, are stunned.
I have stepped out of my crib
in the room set apart from theirs
to show myself an old man
in their youth.

I cannot spare them;
I tell them grief is pure
in what there is to know
between birth and death.

I take their hands
and lead them in a circle,
locking eyes, hands, bodies
with the past in our future.

And Rest

You who gave me birth between your sturdy legs
are dead. You who gave me food and drink
and washed my clothes, ironed my shirts,
took me shopping for a suit and coat are dead.
Now that I am old I sing you back
to stay with me, companion that you were to me
in youth, as now I gather strength to come
to where you are and rest with you.

Father

Father fell backwards off the stool
and as they picked him up,
already paralyzed,
he smiled apologetically.

Every once in a while
I remember he is alive
and it amazes me: I have been
living as if alone in the world
with no one to turn to for advice
or a lecture, and yet my father
aged and dry—what could he say
to me but to show himself
in his brittle bones
as if saying,
I've had my day.

Sky

I would be buried beside my parents
to be told, Yes, our darling son,
it could have been better,
but we loved you. Lie down
beside us, face up to the sky.

Separate Rooms

We are an aging couple
in a house surrounded
by silence, left
to ourselves to do with
our lives as we wish
in the security of our persons,
to act as we had wanted to
since youth—freely
and spontaneously
towards one another,
given our lives'
long wish in old age,
lying in separate beds
in separate rooms.

Knowledge

Lying between her legs,
he was performing an obeisance.
It was his known self,
certainly not intended
to create a child, nor to make sex
the existence. There would be
transformations of his bones and body
in regal time, time that was this
thrusting towards the sadness
of climax within an aperture
of flesh, as she who lay beneath him
heaved towards what they sought
in common and that would bring them
to such pleasure as to obliterate,
at least for then,
the knowledge of their future death.

If We Could Be Brought

If we could be brought to the surface
like a gleaming fish and served for supper,
if we could eat and swallow our own life
to make a good meal, if we could go fishing
for ourselves and feed on the gleaming
swimmer below the surface of our skin—
the fish that is our slippery life
and death.

A Leaf

Bearing leaves again,
the tree that was the skeleton of itself:
how is it I grow more tired
with each succeeding year
of bringing a poem to life?

I am not content as an old man
growing nearer to myself,
alive on earth,
a leaf in season.

I Close My Eyes

I close my eyes like a good little boy at night in bed,
as I was told to do by my mother when she lived,
and before bed I brush my teeth and slip on my pajamas,
as I was told, and look forward to tomorrow.

I do all things required of me to make me a citizen of sterling worth.
I keep a job and come home each evening for dinner. I arrive at the
same time on the same train to give my family a sense of order.

I obey traffic signals. I am cordial to strangers, I answer my mail promptly. I keep a balanced checking account. Why can't I live forever?

Blessing

Woman, that you know of death is a blessing;
that you love me for what I am,
of this world, and will lay a hand
upon my beating heart.

Longing

This longing to be healed in you
each night in bed without you
is a struggle to breathe.

Forever

At the water's edge of a deserted beach,
standing between the two choices,
I contemplate my position
with an objectivity
as though the mind
lives on forever.

That's the Sum of It

I don't know which to mourn. Both have died on me, my wife and my car. I feel strongly about my car, but I am also affected by my wife. Without my car, I can't leave the house to keep myself from being alone. My wife gave me two children, both of whom, of course, no longer live with us, as was to be expected, as we in our youth left our parents behind. With my car, I could visit my children, when they are not too busy.

Before she died, my wife urged me to find another woman. It's advice I'd like to take up but not without a car. Without a car, I cannot find myself another woman. That's the sum of it.

God's

I must train myself to no longer exist
but as a stone lifted and thrown
to wherever I land, a new place,
a new odor to it and new sound
and action surrounding me, all this
without the thought of loss, despair,
or hope, a preparation for loss.
Such a life would be god's, if one
existed. But it is life I can assume
is god's, and I can live it.

I Live with My Contradictions

I live with my contradictions
intact, seeking transcendence
but loving bread. I shrug
at both and from behind
the summer screen I look
out upon the dark, knowing
death as one form
of transcendence, but
so is life.

Despite the Plainness of the Day

Despite the plainness of the day,
like all other days: the simple sun,
the ordinary wind, the usual trees
and the expected buildings, my cock
in you as I move back and forth
in happiness makes of the plain day
its own festive occasion.

Orgasm

It is the mind experiencing its pleasure,
its own flood, and as the flood recedes
leaves me calm and level as the Midwest plains,
fertile yet still. I rise from this calm
slowly, the way brush grows up silently
on the plains, where no eyes come upon it.
From brush, tall foliage under a permissive sky.
This is how I love my mind.

I walk with it, head held erect,
and I look at others thinking and hoping,
so that we may put our heads together
and hear each other's high, keen note
of pleasure in the self, life singing
to life, more beautiful
even than a single mind.

Opening Paths

I am indifferent again, I am obsessed by indifference. Worried by it. Why indifference after I have discharged my stream of love. There you are, breasts, buttocks and belly lying beside me and I converse with you on Dostoyevsky, Tolstoy, excitedly, intelligently? You listen, absorbed, your eyes wander over my face with detachment. You too have discharged your love and can think and see clearly again. Are we in love? We are in conversation, we have enjoyed our sex. As I talk, I look at your body and do not necessarily need to possess it. Look at your face, it is lived. Age is beginning to tell. You look at my face, age is beginning to tell: lines, jowls. We are middle-aged lovers who can discuss after a grand orgasm together that was the body at work and now the mind, the self-regard which the mind stands for comes into play. Our common interests must be stated, we must find another way of communicating fully besides through body, and we do it with the mind. We search for the fullness of communication and understanding between us. We are wary, unsure, eager to do well, uncertain of each other's mind and knowledge. We will go on to discover everything that can keep us together. We talk, stumble upon the wrong phrase, correct ourselves, wait diffidently for the other to speak, react excitedly in response to convey interest, identify with agreement or a loving disagreement that will stimulate us to speak even more rapidly and concretely. We are opening paths to each other. This is so much more difficult than love and we are trying.

See

It's not you in particular,
not your hair, nor breasts, nor belly,
thigh, voice, and subtly inviting movements.

It is not my asking and not your reply
and not my excitement
nor yours—this movement together
of nearly unendurable pleasure.

See from our bed,
now that we recline and rest,

how the wind lifts up
the unexceptionable waves
and sets them down.

You

You spring from a fantasy
for charm, light, and beauty
I would give myself to
with outspread arms
and in your absence
fall.

My Love for You

My love for you is a dark hall
through which I tap my way
along the walls for an exit
to an orchard under which
I may sit and speak
of my relationship to earth,
like that of the pear or the peach,
eaten for breakfast, filling
a need; desired in the daytime
and in the evening
and praised for its beauty
in the eye and in the mouth.

Each of Us

We shall love each other in bed, parlor, and kitchen
when we two meet as strangers in the guise of clerks,
lawyers, doctors, or what have you
that in no way resembles either you or us,
except that they have the bodies
like our own.

Peace to each of us.
Peace to the strangers.
Let them love each other
as we cannot now.

We write this to tell you
we are guilty
and cannot live without the guilt
and cannot live with it.

Now

He's in class teaching
English Literature and she
is approaching between the aisles
naked, her buttocks flowing,
her legs strutting
their pride in themselves

No one else but he sees her,
which is exactly as he wants it.
She is his private memory,
discussing Chaucer.

She seats herself,
crossing her legs,
brown pubic hair
forming a large dot
below her navel. She
looks at him and smiles,
the enigmatic kind,
as if to say, I'm here,
as you have asked of me.
Now are you at peace?

Blood

Does my blood need a motive
to travel the length of my body,
picking up waste, discharging waste,
taking on health? Do I need
to explain why loving you
is important and why leaving
is equally so, as when my blood
slows, meeting impediments; halts
and dies? You and I have met
to transact some business
between us and my delight
is in measure with our success
and my warmth toward you.
What other meaning can I find
for us, if there be meaning here
as when stars collapse
and new ones are born
out of the same matter?

I Dream I Hurl a Spear

I dream I hurl a spear into the body of my love.
I am brutal, but the spear begins to glow along its shaft
and transfixes me. I stand covered in its radiance,
unable to move, magnetized toward the spear that I reach
out to touch and then grasp and stroke and carry myself
forward along its length until I have touched the body
of my love itself at the point where the spear has entered.
I sob, I shake in convulsions, and the body of my love
bends forward to comfort me as I support myself against
it in a paroxysm of leaving my body.

Midnight II

In place of you
the moon is a presence
in my room I must turn
my back on to sleep
in the dark.

Shapely

He stops his wife in the street
and looks into her bakery bag
for the breakfast delicacies.
The day is Sunday and temperate,
the sun mild. She wears shorts.
Her face is unremarkable,
with a kind of petulant mouth.
In the bag he finds what he is
looking for. They talk together
quickly and lightly and then he
continues up the street and she
resumes her way to the apartment.
Swinging his arms and legs wide,
he walks chipper: his wife has
shapely thighs.

It's Not You I Miss

It's not you I miss
but the weave of thought
around your presence
with which to clothe
the bareness of my life—
a cloth of the colors
of the days and nights
we spent together.

The Love We Had

The love we had for one another is somewhere
missing, unhappy with ourselves
and sad for one another, as if
we have consigned each other to oblivion.

I love you from a distance,
I hear your voice behind a wall
calling me to find a path around,
if but to show myself
at least alive, if not in love
but willing to be seen with you.

Let others think what they may,
we'll have the mask
that fits the face of grief,
at risk among others.

Without Sexual Attraction

Without sexual attraction, there is
the brutal movement of the sea.
The face peers out of its skeletal frame
and hands reach like bone.

Without love, the streets
are hollow sounding
with wooden, hurried steps,
voices like caverns of death.
We pass each other as trains do,
whistling screams.

The Puzzle

All the way to my station I was trying to make out who was the guy responsible. I studied their faces and the kid's, trying to make it out that way. The kid had brown eyes. One of the men had blue eyes, so I figured he was out. But then I remembered that brown eyes always came ahead of blue. I was going on like that all the way to my station. And once I saw one of the men, the one with the kid, listening to a conversation between the other one and the woman, and I thought from the manner in which they addressed him occasionally, with a smile, that he was a friend of the family, after all. But then, goddamn it, after the other had said something about being happy to get back from the trip, the woman holding his hand and smiling at him, I heard the guy with the kid say that he and Margaret—that's what he called the woman—had gotten in some new furniture while the other was away. That's the husband, I said to myself. The guy who said he got in the new furniture. The other is the friend. What the hell! Then I heard this one, the one who had been away, say to the woman, "Uncle told me to send him pictures of the kid, he wants to see his nephew." And the woman kept holding his hand and smiling at him. I was going nuts, really. Well, I had to get off at my station. It doesn't make any difference to me who was the father, maybe both were, the way it looked to me. I mean it doesn't make any difference to me how it happened, but it was puzzling. Suppose it was only one of the men, how in hell were you supposed to know?

The Life

To rest in love as a water bug rests on the surface, swinging to and fro with the gentle rhythm of th tide, then lightly dashing across the surface to catch his yet tinier victim.

What would I dash over the surface for? To catch at my prey, the poem that like the victim of the water bug would affirm my life: to rest in love as on a water bed, with all my frame snugly fitting, and every which way I turn the surface holding me closely. I'd lose my sense of self in this watery support, the self of hip and thigh, my head, too, afloat. Let this be the life of love.

Index of Titles

INDEX OF TITLES

UNIVERSITY PRESS OF NEW ENGLAND publishes books under its own imprint and is the publisher for Brandeis University Press, Brown University Press, University of Connecticut, Dartmouth College, Middlebury College Press, University of New Hampshire, University of Rhode Island, Tufts University, University of Vermont, and Wesleyan University Press.

ABOUT THE AUTHOR

David Ignatow has published fifteen volumes of poetry and three prose collections. Born in Brooklyn, he has lived most of his life in the New York metropolitan area, working as editor of *American Poetry Review* and *Beloit Poetry Journal*, and poetry editor of *The Nation*. He has received the Bollingen Prize, two Guggenheim fellowships, and countless other awards.

LIBRARY OF CONGRESS CATALOGING-IN-PUBLICATION DATA
Ignatow, David, 1914–
Against the evidence : selected poems, 1934–1994 / David Ignatow.
p.   cm. — (Wesleyan poetry)
Includes bibliographical references and index.
ISBN 0–8195–2211–2 (hard). — ISBN 0–8195–1214–1 (pbk.)
I. Title.   II. Title: 6 decades.   III. Series.
PS3517.G53A6   1993
811'.54—dc20   93–4303
∞